Books by John Adair

LEADERSHIP AND MANAGEMENT

Training for Leadership
Training for Decisions
Training for Communication
Action-Centred Leadership
Management and Morality
The Becoming Church
Effective Leadership
Management Decision-Making
Effective Teambuilding
How to Manage Your Time
Not Bosses But Leaders
Developing Leaders
Great Leaders
Understanding Motivation
The Art of Creative Thinking

HISTORY

Hastings to Culloden (with Peter Young)
Roundhead General
Cheriton, 1644
John Hampden
The Pilgrims' Way
Royal Palaces of Britain
Founding Fathers
By the Sword Divided

To Robin,

with best wishes,

John

Christmas, 1990.

The Challenge o

THE
CHALLENGE OF
INNOVATION

John Adair

TALBOT
ADAIR
PRESS

Published by
The Talbot Adair Press
Newlands, Pewley Hill
Guildford, Surrey GU1 3SN, England

ISBN 0 9511835 3 2

Phototypeset by Primagraphics, Camberley.
Printed and bound in Great Britain by
Biddles Ltd, Guildford and King's Lynn

Contents

Introduction

Innovation is the key to winning — and keeping — leadership in world markets. New ideas and new ways of doing things are the main ingredients in sustained business success. But how is the necessary innovation going to be achieved? By whom? That is the theme of this book.

Innovation calls for a special form of creativity, which I call TEAM CREATIVITY. Of course, all organizations are teams — or at least they are potentially so. For the effective production and marketing of goods or services these days — delivery on time, at the required quality and at a competitive price — calls for high-performance teamwork. But to *improve* those existing products and to *develop* new products and services, requires a different order of teamwork — TEAM CREATIVITY.

In brief, those organizations which practise team creativity will survive and prosper; those who do not will probably decline and disappear. The graveyard of business is already littered with companies that could not or would not innovate in the face of inevitable change. Will your organization soon be occupying a place in that graveyard?

If you are quite certain that in ten years' time your organization will be providing *exactly* the same products or services to *exactly* the same customers, then you have no need to read this book. But before you act on that conclusion I suggest you ask six or seven other people in your company — at least four of them under the age of thirty — if they agree with you. They may have some surprises for you. The crew often have a more informed opinion about the seaworthiness of a ship than the captain.

Assuming that you are in the business of innovation then this is the book for you. By the time you have finished reading it you should have:

● a clear understanding of the concepts of innovation and team creativity;

● some sketchmaps or frameworks of what an innovative organization should look like in terms of its philosophy, strategy, management and structure;

● a firm grasp of the nature of team creativity and how individuals can build on one another's ideas;

● some knowledge of how to provide the leadership necessary if team creativity is to flourish;

● the inspiration to become both a creative leader and a creative team member.

If you introduce the team creativity approach into your workplace it will greatly enhance everyone's enjoyment of work. For people get much more out of work if they put their minds fully into it. As Noël Coward said, 'Work is more fun than fun.'

1. What is Innovation?

He that will not apply new remedies must accept new evils: for time is the greatest innovator.

Francis Bacon

To innovate means literally to bring in or introduce something new — some new idea, method or device. The novelty may, of course, be more apparent than real. For newness is a relative term. What is new to me may be already familiar to you. But innovation as a wider concept has certain important facets. In particular it combines two major overlapping processes: having new ideas and implementing them.

INVENTION AND INNOVATION

The first part of this equation — having new ideas — is better indicated by such words as creation or invention. It is the subject of a companion book to this one, entitled *The Art of Creative Thinking*. Because all of us have the mental capacity to synthesize as well as to analyse we can all be taught to be creative at a low level. Rather fewer people — but still a surprisingly large number – indulge in what might properly be called creative thinking. Yet very few of those will produce ideas, creations or inventions which are hailed as both original and of long-lasting value to society.

Not all such new ideas, however potentially useful to society, are actually developed. For in order for the idea to be realized and put to work the PROCESS OF INNOVATION has to occur. Creation, invention or discovery focus upon the *conception* of the idea; innovation covers the whole process whereby the new idea is brought into productive use.

At once you can see that innovation takes us into the realms of organization, money, buildings, management and production, and eventually into society at large. Without this extension into the practical world any new idea will remain just a new idea, lodged in some individual's brain.

It follows that not all creative individuals are innovators, nor are all innovators invariably creative or inventive as individuals. Inventors, for example, can be notoriously impractical and unbusinesslike. They are sometimes robbed of the fruits of their success by unscrupulous entrepreneurs, who take their ideas to market and pay them no proper reward.

CLIVE SINCLAIR: INVENTOR AND INNOVATOR

Sir Clive Sinclair, Britain's leading inventor, is a rare example of an inventor who has had to turn himself into an innovator and entrepreneur. In the early 1970s he began to make his name as an inventor with the 'Executive' pocket calculator and the digital 'Black Watch'. He shot to fame a decade later with his home computers, which made Britain the world leader in that market. Some of Sinclair's greatest successes have been in miniaturization — from the matchbox radio and pocket television to wafer-thin silicon chips. He was also one of the first to see the potential of pocket telephones.

Sinclair firmly believes that in order to be successful the inventor has to turn himself into an innovator. 'You go out there and you start a company and you get your invention off the ground,' he says. 'You have to be an entrepreneur, because there are buckets of ideas around and they're not always very good ones. We don't need any inventors really: most of them are just a nuisance most of the time.'

As an inventor, entrepreneur and manager Sinclair has not enjoyed uninterrupted success. Yet he has made his millions and so he is able to do what he wants most, which is to pursue in freedom his vocation as an inventor.

His career does, however, highlight the distinction between creation and innovation, and it provides a case study of one man's bold and largely successful attempt to bridge the gap between them.

INNOVATION AS INCREMENTAL CHANGE

Innovation is not dependent solely upon new invention. Existing products and services, organizations and institutions, should also undergo change intended to improve them. In this case change is not a quantum leap forward, but a series of steps — some small, some large — in a desired direction.

Innovation, as the introduction of change in this sense, has the essential characteristic of being GRADUAL. It is concerned with the smaller modifications or alterations in what already exists. This kind of incremental change tends to be of little interest to the creative thinker or inventor, who is seeking a more radical break with past tradition or what is presently available.

From this characteristic flows three important consequences. First, it is much more easy to plan for innovation than it is for creation or invention. The latter is highly dependent upon the creative individual, and by its nature cannot be required by a given date or even by any date. That does not mean to say that creativity cannot be encouraged or stimulated by having the right climate or culture in organizations: of course it can. Secondly, innovation is more positive and less threatening than other forms of change. Thirdly, everyone — managers and staff — can be fully involved in innovation. Let us briefly consider each of three significant characteristics in turn.

THE MANAGEMENT OF CHANGE

'Observe always that everything is the result of change,' wrote the Roman emperor and philosopher Marcus Aurelius. 'The universe is change.' From the earliest days of history men and women have been aware of both CHANGE and CONTINUITY as the key elements in their experience of life. Indeed, if life is like weaving a pattern on the loom of time, then change and continuity are its warp and weft.

Wise men have always known that you should not ignore change for you cannot stop it happening. 'We must obey the greatest law of change,' said Edmund Burke. 'It is the most powerful law of nature.' This act of acceptance is the first step towards exercising control over change.

But can you really MANAGE change? Not entirely, it must

be admitted. We experience change as something that is happening in the world, and as something that is perhaps happening to us personally or to the organization we work for. As creative and innovative individuals, or as members of innovative organizations, we are also sources or agents of change. Waters from our springs or streams feed the sea of change. Change begets change, and so the volume and pace of change — technological, social, political and economic – increases. No wonder that some people fear that change will get out of hand.

The Latin word for 'hand', incidentally, is *manus*, and it is the root of our English word *manage*. Originally it was applied to handling things in the sense of controlling their movement towards desired ends. Thus a few centuries ago men could talk about managing a warhorse or a ship at sea, or managing a sword in a duel, or managing an army in the field.

It was then applied to managing institutions and businesses. It makes sense to talk about managing money, for money is a thing. But its application to people – in such phrases as 'man-management' or 'the management of people' — is more problematic. For people are not things. People need to be led and motivated, rather than managed.

When it comes to managing change in an organization the chief executive and senior management team should be able to sense the drift of change, and make sure that their organization is aligned with it. That requires a sense of direction and also considerable powers of leadership in order to keep people moving together along the same path of change.

In some cases, in order to achieve this sense of movement dictated by the tides and winds of change, it is necessary to change people's attitudes. For it is essential that attitudes are right. If you do not take change by the hand, you can be sure that it will take you by the throat.

While innovation is a natural human activity, in the context of organizational life it should be both intentional and planned as far as possible. If you fail to plan YOU PLAN TO FAIL. It stems from a universal acceptance of the fact that an organization which does not confront change, or sees no need to innovate, will stagnate, decay and eventually die. Trees begin to die from the top downwards, and so this sorry process usually stems from the chief executive and those around him or her. Hence, in

Chapter Six, we shall look searchingly at the leadership of the chief executive in changing organizations.

All innovations, then, are changes, but not all changes are innovations. An innovation is a deliberate and specific introduction of what is new, aimed at accomplishing the goals of the organization more effectively. Innovation of this kind does not happen by accident. It calls for good leadership and management at all levels of the organization.

INNOVATION IS POSITIVE

Major change may come as a challenge to some people, but it comes as a threat to others. The temper of innovation is less threatening, however, simply because it does not introduce itself in the guise of the dramatically different. Initially it is not a complete transformation of the system. Incremental innovation, it is true, may mount up eventually to something much bigger. Indeed, it may reach the point where the purpose or identity of the organization are called into question. That may lead in turn to radical reform, or it may result in another organization's being set up.

But the spirit of innovation is evolutionary rather than revolutionary. As the Japanese proverb puts it: 'I would rather teach one hundred men to take one step forwards than teach one man to take a hundred steps.'

For managing innovation by definition is about making things happen. And if proposed or planned changes arouse too much antagonism, or prove to be unacceptable to a critically large number of people, then they are usually inadvisable. For only unwise leaders try to push change against a sea of determined and sustained opposition. If that happens to you, you have come by the wrong path. But innovation that better satisfies a perceived want, or reduces a sore source of annoyance or complaint, will soon gather a following and win acceptance.

ALL CAN PARTICIPATE

Each person at work has approximately 10,000 million brain cells, together with a full range of mental faculties, notably analysing, synthesizing and valuing abilities. In all of us these processes can take place intentionally on a conscious plane of thought and also — less intentionally and less predictably — in our unconscious minds, giving us insights, intuitions, brainwaves, gut feelings, intimations, daydreams and the occasional pearl of a genuinely new idea.

As a general principle people with a 'hands-on' involvement in any product or service — providing they have a modicum of interest in their work — will tend to have new ideas for doing it better. These will usually, but not always, be quite small or incremental improvements. But they are a vital part of the general process of innovation. Given encouragement and a listening leadership, this natural harvest of ideas can be increased dramatically. Any truly innovative organization should have, in Sinclair's phrase, 'buckets of ideas' available if it sets up some simple systems for lowering the buckets into the well and drawing them up.

Interest leads to ideas. In turn, the recognition of ideas by management leads to more job interest, greater involvement and deeper commitment. Even if — for good reasons that are explained — a team member's proposals are not acceptable, or, if acceptable cannot be implemented, there is no loss of motivation. The important thing from the motivational perspective is the feeling of being really part of the enterprise, with a full share of responsibility in developing the quality of the product or service. Identification matters more than the fate of any particular suggestion.

KEY POINTS

● Innovation is more than having new ideas: it includes the process of successfully introducing them or making things happen in a new way. It turns ideas into useful, practicable and commercial products or services.

● As Nature illustrates, most change happens gradually. Innovation encompasses this gradual improvement of existing ideas and forms, products and services as well as the marketing of new inventions or creations. Like snowballs, these changes soon add up to a programme of continuous innovation.

● Programmes of useful change call for managerial leaders. Change throws up the need for leaders; leaders tend to bring about change. Although innovation is a natural process it is much more effective if it is properly led. That means that it must be welcomed, planned for, controlled, monitored, and, above all, guided towards the ends of the organization.

● Avoid change for change's sake, for it rarely pays off. Thoughtless alteration or modification can lead to a loss of core quality in a product or service. 'Striking to be better,' wrote Shakespeare, 'oft we mar what is well.'

● Few of us can or should become professional creative thinkers, such as inventors, artists, composers or authors, but we can all participate in the team creativity of innovation. Each part or role in the drama of turning ideas into useful reality calls for creativity, imagination, experience and ingenuity.

The business of life is to go forwards.
Samuel Johnson

2. The Conditions for Successful Innovation

*What's the secret of entrepreneurial success?
It's knowing how to use OPB (other
people's brains) and OPM (other people's
money).*

*J. B. Fuqua
Chairman, Fuqua Industries Inc.*

Does your organization have a strategy for change? In particular, has it given strategic consideration to creating the necessary conditions for innovation?

The challenge of improving the quality, reliability and performance of products and services while being competitive on price actually calls for a dual strategy. First, continuous change designed to improve productivity and profitability of existing products has to be planned. Secondly, there has to be a strategy for introducing new or better products. Although no magic formulas exist, there are six necessary climatic conditions which enable innovation to flourish. You may like to give your organization a mark out of ten for each of these six characteristics as you read this chapter.

MANAGEMENT COMMITMENT

'Change? That's the last thing we want around. Things are bad enough already.' The manager who made that remark certainly lacked any commitment to planned, innovative change. For too many managers are merely reactive to change. They change only when they have to do so. 'Too little and too late' is often the epitaph you will read on their monuments in that graveyard of failed companies I mentioned earlier.

Some managers acknowledge the need for change in a general sense, but they don't accept the practical implications for themselves and their companies. 'Everyone likes innovation,' said Walter Wriston, Chairman of First National City Bank, 'until it affects himself, and then it's bad.'

Such managers are like little Napoleons. For Napoleon once declared to his marshals: 'One must change one's tactics every ten years if one wishes to maintain one's superiority.' *But he did not follow his own advice.* His tactics were so predictable at Waterloo that he gave Wellington an enormous competitive advantage. It enabled Wellington to end the career of his great adversary.

The writing that spells out the importance of managing change before it manages you has been on the wall now for some time in the hard school of experience. A spate of books has also shouted out the message. 'An established company which in an age demanding innovation is not capable of innovation is doomed to decline and extinction,' predicted management sage Peter F. Drucker many years ago. 'And a management which in such a period does not know how to manage innovation is incompetent and unequal to its task. Managing innovation will increasingly become a challenge to management, and especially to top management, and a touchstone of its competence.'

The top leadership team — the chief executive and executive directors — need to show visibly and audibly that they are committed to the dual strategy of positive innovation outlined above. Their weight and influence is necessary to overcome the barriers and resistances to useful change which innovators often encounter. For the process of innovation may become too slow if vested interests are allowed their head. What may seem to you a corporate opportunity may be perceived by others as a departmental threat. It is your job as a leader at any level in the organization to facilitate desirable change and to encourage that attitude throughout the management team.

POSITIVE STRATEGIC THINKING

A corporate strategy should answer the following questions:

● What business are we in?

● Where are we now?

● Where do we want to be in three to five years' time?

● Where might we be in ten years' time?

● What are our strengths and weaknesses?

● Have we the resources to implement our strategic plans?

● What might be the main threats from our competitors?

● Have we a capability for dealing with the unexpected or the unknown?

These questions are deceptively simple. For, as Clausewitz pointed out, 'What needs to be done in war is simple, but in war it is very difficult to do simple things.' Business is certainly like war in that respect.

Getting the right answer to the first question in the above list is especially important. It is not easy. If you make it too general you run the risk of losing sight of your particular niche of excellence. If you make it too specific, on the other hand, you may eliminate areas for creative development and innovation.

The American company O. M. Scott, it is reported, spent a year deciding between two core mission statements: 'to make fertilizers' or 'to keep lawns green'. They finally chose the second purpose. It led to investment in facilities to produce a variety of chemicals and implements to keep lawns green. Such product diversification would not have been consistent with their traditional assumption that they were in the business of producing fertilizers.

The last question in the above list is also important in the context of innovation. A wise general keeps a reserve in order to respond to the unforeseen, and so should a chief executive. That contingency may be an unexpected market shift or the sudden emergence of a new technology. Having a corporate strategy should therefore include the provision for an uncommitted reserve, a capability in terms of human and material resources to respond to unpredictable (but not improbable) future opportunities or necessities.

Above all, innovation should not be a reactive process but part of a strategy that gives direction. It needs to be fed by the dynamo of a corporate sense of purpose. Such a strategy will balance the present needs of producing and marketing *existing* goods and services — the commercial priority — with the middle-term and long-term requirement of *research and development*. A balanced and coherent strategy will enable your organization to build on its past successes and create its desired future. *It is the only sure pathway to profitable growth.*

A LONG-TERM PERSPECTIVE

The criterion of short-term profit — the bottom line each quarter — is clearly inappropriate when it comes to developing and introducing new products and services. 'No great thing is created suddenly,' wrote the Roman philosopher Epictetus, 'any more than a bunch of grapes or a fig. If you tell me that you desire a fig, I answer you that there must be time. Let it first blossom, then bear fruit, then ripen.' So it is with any commercially-viable new product or service.

In comparison with Japan, for example, where banks and corporations take a more long-term view, Western financial institutions and share-holders in such countries as Britain and the United States, are notorious for their *short-termism*. Such purblind thinking and policy-making cannot encourage industry to innovate. Banks in particular in these threatened countries need to recover a larger purpose than mere short-term profit. For they exist in part to provide a service to business and industry, who are the engine-room of their economies. Too often they fail to do so. At least they should now adjust their sights to take a more medium-term view — the good old British compromise — when deciding on the investments they should make for the future.

British entrepreneurs Peter de Savary, Richard Branson and

Andrew Lloyd Webber are among those who recently have bought their public companies back into private ownership. They resent what they see as too much emphasis on producing short-term profits at the expense of long-term growth. 'Being private enables us to adopt the Japanese approach of building market share slowly and then waiting for profits,' says Branson. 'Most of the year, running a public company, was spent worrying about next year's profits. Since going private, I haven't once asked for a profit forecast.'

But risk-averse financial institutions should not be made into scapegoats. Industry's *own* commitment of money to research and development must also be examined. Where do you stand in this particular league table in relation to your principal domestic competitors? How does your national average of industrial investment in research and development compare with that of other nations' industries? It is important to know the answers to these questions. For, as the proverb says, 'If you are not part of the solution, you are part of the problem.'

RESPONSIVENESS TO CHANGE

Some organizations suffer from hardening of the arteries and stiffening of the joints. Some of these victims are still young when this creeping disease of organizational arthritis hits them. They gradually become rigid and inflexible. Addicted to the well-tried formula, they become steadily and unconsciously more averse to the new and unfamiliar. Increasing inflexibility in attitude and practice eventually makes any sort of improvement seem initially too costly. The subsequent lack of positive change that stems from this attitude can usually be rationalized in such excuses as 'it's too expensive' or 'we are successful already — why change?' It is important to remember that this organizational disease is entirely self-inflicted.

Flexibility is becoming the key quality of the truly innovative organization. The flexible person, team or organization is capable of responding or conforming to changing or new situations. That places a high premium on communication. Barriers between staff people in different areas need to be minimized. Keep open the communication channels between researchers and production people, between researchers and market people, and between researchers and the customer.

In organizational terms that also means flattening the hierarchical pyramid and pushing decision-making downwards or outwards to where the organization interacts with its environment. In short, it means to create an entrepreneurial and matrix-type management structure while preserving the efficient monitoring system and disciplines essential in any large organization.

In a flexible and open organization adjustments to new developments and changes are quickly made. There is an intense curiosity about everything. Problems are broken into their component parts, relationships among variables are understood and fundamental aspects and critical parts of a problem are grasped. Usually there is more than one feasible solution or way forwards. So that if one solution or course doesn't work out a different approach is soon developed and implemented.

The importance of *structures* for growth can hardly be stressed enough. They should assure innovators both support and stimulation. The former Chairman and Chief Executive of 3M Lewis W. Lehr explains how that remarkably innovative company is structured for organic growth:

'With about forty product divisions, various projects and departments, and about fifty overseas companies, 3M has close to one hundred major profit centres. Yet each one must feel much like a free-standing business. Basically, division managers run their own shops. They make their own decisions, develop their own new products — and take responsibility for the consequences. As teams within a division develop successful new products and businesses, division management is responsible for spinning them off into self sustaining enterprises. We call this process "divide and grow". Our policy of dividing for growth is based on a discovery made years ago. We found that when a division reaches a certain size, it may spend too much time on established products and markets. It then has less time to spend on new products and business. When we break out a new business, we appoint a new management team. We give people an opportunity to identify with the new business. And we find, almost without exception, that the new unit begins to grow at a faster rate.

'Take, for example, our tape business. From our original Scotch brand masking tape and transparent tape have come four separate divisions, with countless lines of tape for industrial, commercial,

and home use. Also out of our tape laboratories came a new
surgical tape and surgical drape in the 1950s. These products gave
birth to our health care business and eventually to our Medical,
Surgical, and Orthopaedic Products Divisions. And out of those
same labs came a line of electrical-grade tapes. These in their
turn spawned several divisions specializing in electrical connectors,
terminals, insulation, and so forth. Our corporate structure is
specifically designed to encourage innovators to take an idea and
run with it. If they succeed, they may find themselves running
their own business under the 3M umbrella.'

ACCEPTANCE OF RISK

It is virtually impossible to innovate without accepting an
element of risk. You can and should calculate risk and adjust
your exposure to match your resources. But you cannot *eliminate*
risk and still see yourself or your organization as being creative
and innovative. 'Nothing ventured, nothing gained.'

The downsides of risk are mistakes and failure. In any entrepreneurial and innovative enterprise there will be such failures.
They are, of course, quite different from the failures that arise
from indecision and inaction. Business leaders must accept this
downside and pick up the bill bravely. The possibility of failure
should not be used as an excuse — it often happens — to pull
in the horns of creative thinking and innovation.

There should be a post mortem after each failure — in order
to learn the lessons, not to award the punishments. Usually you
will discover that there were some warning signs of impending
failure that were ignored. One important lesson to be learnt from
such post mortems is that managers should face the unpleasant
task of ending potential failures before they gather too much
momentum.

'There are risks and costs to a programme of action,' said John
F. Kennedy. 'But they are far less than the long-range risks and
costs of comfortable inaction.' In other words, if you take risks
you may make mistakes, but if you do not take risks you are
doomed to failure.

Again, Lewis W. Lehr has some wise things to say about the
need to accept mistakes — but only if they are first-time ones.

The corporate culture of 3M has a clear policy or tradition on the matter:

> 'The cost of failure is a major concern for innovators — since that is what will happen to most of them at one time or another. We estimate at 3M that about sixty percent of our formal new-product programmes never make it. When this happens, the important thing is not to crucify the people involved. They should know that their jobs are not in jeopardy if they fail. Otherwise, too many would-be innovators will give in to the quite natural temptation to play it safe. Few things will choke innovation more quickly than the threat of losing a job if you fail.
>
> 'We have a tradition of accepting honest mistakes and failures without harsh penalties. We see mistakes as a normal part of business and an essential by-product of innovation. But we expect our mistakes to have originality. We can afford almost any mistake once. Those who choose to lead high-risk, new-product programmes know that their employment will not be threatened. This attitude of management eliminates one of the major barriers to innovation in large companies.'

As any business grows, it becomes necessary to delegate responsibility and to encourage people to use their initiative. That means allowing people to do their own jobs in their own way. If the person is essentially right, the mistakes that he or she makes are not as serious as would be the great mistake of trying to specify in an autocratic way how everything should be done or to insist on all decisions being made at head office. A top management that is destructively critical when mistakes occur will smother initiative and enterprise. When that happens — goodbye profitable growth.

THE RIGHT INTERNAL ENVIRONMENT

The previous five factors are all contributors to the right culture or climate in which new ideas can be hatched and significant changes implemented.

Apart from tending to have a fluid and organic rather than a rigid and mechanistic form, innovative organizations encourage participation in decision-making, problem-solving and creative thinking. They have policies or guidelines rather than rules, keeping the latter to the minimum. They have good internal communications, more by word of mouth than by memo or letter. No one expects deferential behaviour, but people do respect their colleagues — including their leaders. 'Bosses demand respect; leaders earn respect.'

The difficulty, of course, is to combine these ingredients in the corporate culture which favours new ideas and innovation with the high degree of structure, discipline and routine that is required to manufacture products and deliver a proper customer service. Not all members of the organizational team will be equally capable in both aspects of the business. But then the essential characteristic of a team is that it is composed of people with complementary temperaments, sets of qualities, interests, knowledge, and skills.

KEY POINTS

● 'If the trumpet give an uncertain sound, who shall prepare himself to the battle?' The top management team should seek ways of making their commitment to positive and useful change visible to all concerned.

● Strategic thinking is an escape from the tyranny of the present. It leads you to think in more general terms about the desired future. Are you a leader for tomorrow as well as today?

● If an army marches on its stomach then a business marches on its investments. Research and development is the seedcorn for future innovation. It is not a cost but an investment, one with no predictable outcome. Is your organization making that investment?

● Flexibility is the ability — personal as well as corporate — for modifying, altering and perhaps radically changing what you are doing. Rigid or inflexible structures produce inertia.

● Risk is the brother of innovation. As the Japanese proverb says: 'Unless you enter the tiger's den you cannot take the cubs.'

● Relaxed, informal relationships encourage innovation, while routine deadens it.

● The results of yesterday's innovations have to be manufactured, marketed and sold. If you do not create a satisfied customer today you can create nothing tomorrow.

It takes genius and courage to originate, not imitate.
Anon

3. Organizing for Team Creativity

*The working of great institutions is mainly
the result of a vast mass of routine, petty
malice, self-interest, carelessness and sheer
mistake. Only a residual fraction is thought.*
George Santayana

When you *organize* anything you impose upon it sequential or spatial form, or both. People or things are put together; they are fitted into their proper place in relation to one another.

The end result of the human activity of organizing is often an *organization*: a complex structure of interdependent and subordinate elements whose relations and properties are largely determined by their function in the whole. The most common metaphor for such man-made organisms is the human body. That analogy gives us such words as *member, head* and *corporate* (from the Latin verb 'to make into a body').

ORDER AND FREEDOM

All organizations are compromises between order and freedom. Our desire to order, and our willingness to accept order, is part of our social nature. Pragmatically we know that unless we cooperate with one another, accept some common procedures and play the part assigned to us, *nothing much will get done*. Order reduces confusion. It makes the successful accomplishment of some common tasks more likely. By submitting to order, however, we give up some of our personal freedom. It is part of the investment we make in any corporate enterprise. We hope, of course, that the rewards will be ample repayment.

Now serious creative thinking demands a great deal of freedom. The less constraints you are under — subjective or objective — the better. Although creative thinking is much more of a social activity than most people imagine, creative thinkers are often markedly individualistic. They are also often rather solitary, more by necessity than temperamental preference. They need fairly long periods of time on their own. Nor can they always predict when they will need to be alone with their thoughts. This is why creative thinkers do not tend to make good organizational men or women.

But without such talented or gifted individuals organizations will not develop significantly new ideas. You can see the classic dilemma. Without creative thinking there will be no strategic innovation. But creative thinkers either do not want to belong to organizations or find that when they do join them their creativity is diminished or restricted by the constraints imposed by organizational life.

INTEGRATING CREATIVITY INTO INDUSTRY

Broadly speaking, there are two ways of solving the problem, which are not mutually incompatible. First, research and development — as creative thinking is called in industry — can be hived off into separate organizations. Most major companies, for example, have their research establishments. These can interact with one another and with the powerhouses for new ideas funded by government, such as national research laboratories and universities.

Good communication between researchers within a large group of companies is essential, for many creative developments can take place by linking up technologies that others see as separate. The former Chairman and Chief Executive of 3M, stresses its importance:

'A pervasive element of our climate of innovation is *communication* — a constant flow of good information in our technical community. It is hard to overestimate the value of communication in a multinational company. We are a highly diversified organization, to say the least. We have about forty separate divisions. We have about eighty-five basic technologies. And we have literally tens of thousands of individual products. Because our product divisions are fairly autonomous, it is natural for technical people to stay squirrelled away in their own labs, concentrating only on their division's technologies.

'To prevent this kind of isolation, we maintain a massive and continuing effort to promote cross-communication among the various innovators. Through an organization called the Technical Forum, our people are in continuing dialogue with one another. The Technical Forum has more than two dozen chapters and committees. In one year they staged more than 160 events, with presentations ranging from "ion implantation in metals and ceramics" to "new therapeutic approaches to rheumatoid arthritis."

'Some of our scientists speak of a kind of super-technology — the ability to combine two or more separate technologies into a unique application or product. The well-developed communications network in 3M's technical community often provides such opportunities. For example, our pavement markings combine retro-reflective technologies and pressure-sensitive adhesive technologies. And our Controltac films for fleet graphics are a combination of glass bubble, adhesive, and imaging technologies. We try to provide incentives and opportunities for innovators to discuss their ideas with kindred spirits and to reinforce one another.'

The second approach is to endeavour to make your whole organization into an innovative one. If you succeed it will be a much less hostile environment for creative thinkers. You can contain and manage creativity within it instead of having to farm it out. Though 3M does have its own research laboratories it is clear that it sees them as only spearheads of a general innovative advance across a broad front of the organization's life.

There are pros and cons for both approaches. Creative and non-creative people are like oil and water: they do not always mix well. 'Managing and innovation do not always fit comfortably together,' adds Lehr. 'That's not surprising. Managers are people who like order. They like forecasts to come out as planned. In fact, managers are often judged on how much order they produce. Innovation, on the other hand, is often a disorderly process. Many times, perhaps most times, innovation does not turn out as planned. As a result, there is tension between managers and innovators.'

To separate the functions of creating and developing new products or services from the functions of production, marketing and accounting — in the sense of having them take place in different organizations or sub-organizations within the group — does therefore offer to solve a lot of problems. It still leaves the possibility of the more commercial sides of the organization employing managers and work people who can suggest detailed and more incremental improvements in existing products and services, and actively encouraging them to do so.

The specialist research organizations — as we may call them — for their part are relieved of the necessary disciplines and systems required for day-to-day manufacturing, distributing and selling, together with some of the financial controls needed to monitor the efficiency and profitability of a commercial enterprise. But they have their own problems, not merely those that stem from managing their own budgets. If they are to be effective — especially in the fields of science and technology — they have to become large. Sheer size, together with the need for financial accountability for the range of materials and the numbers of people involved, breeds — yes, you have guessed it — organization. And organization is antithetical to creativity. For organization in turn can breed bureaucracy, and bureaucracy kills creativity.

GETTING THE BALANCE RIGHT

There is a general trend for research organizations to become more like businesses, while at the same time industrial organizations are beginning to take on a more creative and innovative role. There are, of course, natural limits to both these processes which wise leaders will recognize and respect. It is part of their key responsibility to remind their organizations from time to time what they are there for.

It is easy to construct a continuum of organizations according to their relative involvement in the conception and development of new ideas thus:

You will notice that the diagonal line does not meet the corner intersection. In other words, no organization today is *wholly* creative or *completely* productive. The latter cannot be the case; partly because organizations employ people, and people by their nature cannot avoid thinking, and thinking in turn leads to new ideas; and partly because an organization which *solely* interested itself in reproducing existing goods and services, regardless of

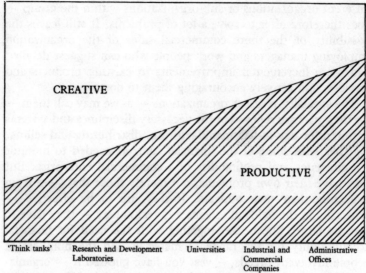

Fig. 3.1 *The Creative/Productive Continuum*

technological or market change, would soon — as we have seen — go out of existence.

No 'creative' organization, on the other hand, can exist without producing something of use or value. It may not employ industrial processes, still less mass production methods, but it is producing outputs. Although it may not be in the business of making profits, it is almost certainly in the business of managing costs. Therefore it has to adopt policies and procedures designed to make the most productive use of the resources at its disposal. That will give it a degree of production-orientation.

LEADERSHIP FOR INNOVATION

It follows from this analysis that the direction of research or ideas-oriented institutions does call for the distinctive qualities of leadership, coupled with management knowledge and abilities — especially in the areas of management finance and marketing (remembering that you have to market your services *within* a large group or organization as well as to outside potential clients).

Equally, it is plain that in order to transform a conservative, dull, partially successful (thanks to yesterday's innovations), rather bureaucratic and inward-looking company, staffed by managers steeped in that culture, into one that is young, dynamic, forward-looking, entrepreneurial and innovative, also calls for a rare combination of leadership and management abilities. Yet that is precisely what President Gorbachev and his colleagues are attempting to do on a grand scale in the Soviet Union today. When it comes to leadership challenge that is like attempting Mount Everest in mid-winter without oxygen. There are lesser summits, however, in less harsh conditions that await their conquerors.

The next two chapters are short case studies. One of the organizations concerned, the Laboratory for Molecular Biology at Cambridge University, lies towards the left-hand end of the above continuum. Your challenge will be to see what factors or features of that highly successful organization for team creativity are transferable to your own organization. The second case study, the Digital Equipment computer company, is an example of a commercial organization which has deliberately and successfully developed an entrepreneurial and innovative philosophy.

KEY POINTS

● Order banishes chaos. Organizing reduces confusion and introduces formality into relationships. But chaos and confusion and informality are the seedbeds of creativity.

● Organizations can delegate or subcontract the work of innovation, in the form of research and development, to specialist units. They can also seek to transform themselves into innovative organizations. These options are not mutually exclusive.

● Any organization falls somewhere on the Creative/Productive continuum. It is important to establish both where you are now and where you want to be on that continuum, for it affects your whole understanding of leadership and management.

● Innovative organizations do not happen by chance. They are the end products of good leadership and management. The essence lies in getting the balance right between freedom and order, between the anatomy of the parts and the integrity of the whole.

● Innovative organizations outside your field of work may hold
secrets for you. Suspend your natural impulse to discard the
experience of others in different walks of life as irrelevant to
your purposes. In this context you can learn from other
organizations which may have a much higher requirement for
creativity than your own. How do they go about organizing
themselves?

> *All establishments die of dignity. They are too*
> *proud to think themselves ill, and to take a*
> *little physic.*
>
> *Sydney Smith*

4. Case Study: The Laboratory of Molecular Biology

Laboratories are the temples of wealth and of the future. There it is that humanity grows, becomes stronger and better.

Louis Pasteur

During the 1980s I conducted a series of some fifteen programmes on leadership and management for university vice-chancellors and heads of departments in the United Kingdom. Those occupying such roles in universities do need some opportunities for reviewing and developing their abilities as leaders. Too often in the past heads of university departments were promoted solely upon their academic record as researchers in their subjects.

'If you are interested in leadership you should go and look at the Medical Research Council's Laboratory of Molecular Biology.' My informant, a participant in one of these seminars, was in fact a senior staff member of the Imperial Cancer Research Fund. He kindly arranged for me to visit the Laboratory and to meet its Director, Dr Sydney Brenner.

The Laboratory of Molecular Biology occupies a rather undistinguished building five storeys high on the outskirts of Cambridge. Yet this is one of the most successful research centres in the world. A few weeks after my visit one of its members, Dr. Cesar Milstein, was awarded a Nobel prize, bringing the number of the Nobel laureates nurtured by the Laboratory to seven.

The double helix structure of the genetic material DNA was first unravelled at the Laboratory by Jim Watson and Francis

Crick. Here the complete structures were worked out for proteins, the other fundamental chemicals of life. The key work on
viruses and chromosomes was also done here. For a laboratory
founded only in 1947 that is a dazzling record of creative science.
'What is your secret?' I asked Dr. Brenner. His answers, I
believe, point to certain principles which apply to all organizations which want to be creative or innovative.

NO CLASS OR HIERARCHICAL DIFFERENCES

After its inception as a two-man operation — Max Perutz and
John Kendrew — the unit which later became the Laboratory
was first housed in Cambridge University's world-renowned
Cavendish Laboratory. When it moved to its own building, Max
Perutz, as the new Laboratory's first chairman, had an opportunity to realize his ideas about how creative work should be
organized. 'One was that there shouldn't be any class differences,' Perutz had said. 'At the Cavendish, scientists and technicians had their tea in different places. I didn't want any hier-
archies or titles.' Brenner told me that he had preserved that
tradition so clearly established by Perutz, the founding architect
of the Laboratory.

Thus the present canteen on the top floor is used by everybody
for tea or coffee breaks as well as for lunch. Here they can
exchange ideas across the formica-topped tables. Random contacts that happen there are regarded as very important. Therefore
the canteen remains open all day. In order to be creative, incidentally, such conversations should not be narrowly focussed on
present-day concerns, or even upon the subject itself. 'I shared
a room with Francis Crick for twenty years,' Sydney Brenner
mentioned to me. 'At least two hours a day we talked nonsense
about anything.'

Individual offices are rare. 'The great difficulty in laboratories
is to get people to collaborate,' Perutz had said. 'If people have
their own offices which they lock up at night, and their own
budgets, they tend not to work together. They worry about
whose budget should be contributing most. So we decided on
the minimum number of offices, and big labs, and as many
shared facilities as possible to throw people together.' Again,

as Dr. Brenner told me, he had decided to perpetuate these arrangements.

Working side by side, chemists learn from microbiologists how to grow the bacteria and viruses they need for their experiments; biologists find out from chemists how to carry out complicated syntheses. When, for example, Frederick Sanger's work on the structure of genetic material became so complex that he needed to use computers, another group of scientists made available to him a specialist in computer work from within their own number.

In the Laboratory there is an emphasis on informality. Everyone was on first name terms, including the Director. The lack of hierarchical structure helped here, for the senior people were no more than 'first among equals' as the leaders and managers of their small research teams. All this serves to encourage cross-boundary work. There is a minimal amount of paperwork, too, and business as far as possible is transacted by word-of-mouth.

LEADING BY EXAMPLE

Unlike management the concept of leadership implies that the leader is producing his or her own output as well as co-ordinating or guiding the work of others. Morale at the Laboratory clearly benefits from the fact that the senior staff are still doing experimental research, not sitting behind desks and managing researchers. 'In the United States,' said Brenner, 'senior people are out of active work by the time they're 35 and running big groups. We aren't.' Brenner, like Perutz his predecessor, believed in being a 'hands-on' researcher.

There is a definite benefit here for young scientists, who have the opportunity to work alongside the masters in their field. As Brenner said to me, 'Science is still like a medieval guild of masters and apprentices.' The Laboratory does no teaching as such — it is purely for research — but undoubtedly it is a place where a lot of learning occurs.

Clearly considerable powers of leadership are required, however, to balance the very competitive nature of scientists at this level with the need for co-operation. But, as all stores are held in common and not allocated to departments, the small teams of scientists and their leaders have to sell their ideas to win their share of the resources. The structure — or lack of it — does not allow them to operate without winning co-operation from their colleagues. As only people are appointed who are willing to impart or teach their technology to others, that climate is self-perpetuating.

Brenner contrasted this approach with what he called 'chateau science'. (In the First World War, Field Marshal Sir Douglas Haig had directed operations well back from the frontline from his General Headquarters in a French chateau, rarely if ever visiting the front line trenches.) Brenner is firmly against the remote control of science by managers. He argued that the director of such an organization as the Laboratory of Molecular Biology should always combine leadership with management.

THE OPTIMUM USE OF RESOURCES

The Laboratory deploys a substantial budget. 'We've been very well and generously funded by the Medical Research Council in a way that makes very long-term projects possible,' Brenner told me. 'There are very few administrators here, so the money is almost all available for research.' Budgetary control is kept to the minimum. 'If things are difficult,' the Director continued, 'I ask people to take it easy. If there is spare money available, I let them know. People really do respond to an appeal to their community sense.' It is always important, if you are a leader, to show that you trust people.

The organizational structure of the Laboratory is designed to facilitate co-operation. There are no departments on the old university model, which so often breed 'departmentalism'. The research is done by many groups or 'loose gangs', each containing fewer than a dozen people under the leadership of one of the more permanent scientific staff. The groups generate their own research programmes and they collaborate at all levels, ranging from scientific discussion to the sharing of equipment and other technical resources. The groups are associated into divisions, but all major decisions of finance and scientific policy are taken jointly by the Heads of Division and the Director, who is responsible for the Laboratory to the Medical Research Council. There is no committee structure beyond the Executive Committee, nor are decisions made by majority vote. Voting creates factions. So leadership is needed to identify or create consensus wherever possible. This structure is not one that eliminates the 'baronial rights' mentality altogether — an impossible task — but it certainly militates against it. People can still be defensive over, for example, appointments. No one is guaranteed anything except their own space. 'The Stores will give you anything,' said Brenner. 'If you fail you do so because of yourself, not through any lack of resources. That reduces the *if only* excuse — "If only I had twenty more pipettes I would have won a Nobel prize."

'If you break the organization down into entities,' continued Brenner, 'no one can get a concept of strategy. Separate units would disintegrate the place. If you want to innovate, give a person a chance. Innovation is gambling. Once you play it safe you are lost.' It has to be a long-term approach. Nobel prize-winner Frederick Sanger, for example, did not publish a research paper for the first eight years while he was at the Laboratory.

THE HUMAN RESOURCE

How are people recruited to the Laboratory? Mainly by informal means, such as recommendation. There used to be no fixed number of people: the governing body appointed people to permanent posts and they in turn made the temporary appointments. Complete outsiders rarely entered at a senior level. 'Most of them came here young,' said Brenner. 'They often went away and returned, but there are very few without a long history of connection.' Success breeds success. Young people acquired the culture of the Laboratory and it became self-propagating. The visiting scientists, who far outnumber the permanent scientific staff, help to prevent intellectual stagnation.

A potential difficulty at the Laboratory is a common one to young entrepreneurial organizations: as they grow older so the staff grow older too. Most of the senior scientific staff at the Laboratory joined in the 1960s when universities were expanding rapidly. Since then the economic climate has changed. Tighter budgets have restricted the number of new recruits. But the practice of academic tenure which gave academics virtually complete job security — now thankfully on the way out — does not sit well with the needs of a creative and innovative organization.

Intuition plays a part in selection. 'I go much by people-feel,' said Brenner. He added that he tried to interview everyone who

came to work at the Laboratory. Incidentally, the part that
intuition plays in creative scientific research itself — quite apart
from selecting people for it — is now much more widely recognized. 'Looking back on my own scientific work,' wrote Lord
Adrian, another Cambridge University scientist who won a Nobel
prize, 'I should say that it shows no great originality but a certain
amount of business instinct which leads to the selection of a
profitable line.'

CREEPING BUREAUCRACY

Dr. Brenner identified creeping bureaucracy as a threat. In the
early days, for example, it was comparatively easy for technicians
to be promoted onto the scientific staff on grounds of demon-
strated ability, even if they had no degree. Medical Research
Council rules now make this impossible. But creative or innovative people do not always shine academically early in their
careers. Nor is early and successful specialization necessarily a
good thing, as the case of Francis Crick illustrates.

The first success in the Laboratory of Molecular Biology came in
1953, when James Watson and Francis Crick discovered the double
helical structure of DNA, which explains the nature of the genetic
information and the way that information is copied and passed on
from parent to progeny. This discovery transformed the face of
biology. In 1945, when he was almost thirty, Crick had taken
stock of his qualifications: 'A not-very-good degree, redeemed
somewhat by my achievements at the Admiralty. A knowledge of
certain restricted parts of magnetism and hydrodynamics, neither
of them subjects for which I felt the least bit of enthusiasm. No
published papers at all . . . Only gradually did I realize that this
lack of qualification could be an advantage. By the time most
scientists have reached the age of thirty they are trapped in their
own expertise. They have invested so much effort in one particular
field that it is often extremely difficult, at that time in their careers,
to make a radical change. I, on the other hand, knew nothing,
except for a basic training in somewhat old-fashioned physics and
mathematics and an ability to turn my hand to new things.' (From
What Mad Pursuit: A Personal View of Scientific Discovery, 1988.)

There are other manifestations of incipient bureaucracy, such as
tighter financial control. 'We even have minutes of meetings

now,' said one senior scientist some two years before my visit. Of course, some degree of organization and some systems of administration are essential. But do they get in the way of what you are there to do?

As Sydney Brenner told me, the Laboratory was run on tradition, not rules. The fact that the Laboratory was originally established to tackle molecular biology was crucially important in determining its ethos. In the face of the brand-new subject they were all initially, as it were, amateurs: the subject itself had no rules. There were no distinctive specialists, and so no claims could be stated for specialist departments. As disciplines became more specialized, however, this advantage began to disappear. Moreover, the Laboratory had enjoyed the benefits of constant expansion. But the need for systems — and less people-dependence — eventually became apparent as expansion slowed down. Brenner, for example, who was appointed Director in 1979, soon afterwards installed the first financial systems.

Inevitably such systems tend to breed accountants and administrators, who can — if one is not careful — see their role as telling leaders and teams what they cannot do. The natural response of a leader, Sydney Brenner said, in an innovative organization, is to retort: 'It's not your job to tell me what I cannot do. Tell me how I can find a way to bend the rules in order to make it happen.'

Size, together with systems, leads to greater pressure to introduce middle levels of management. At the date of my visit the Laboratory had resisted such a step. It had even phased out some incipient layers of middle-management which made their appearance in the 1960s.

The extraordinary culture of the Laboratory of Molecular Biology, which has made it one of the best places in the world to do advanced scientific research, is actually very fragile. That is true of the culture in any innovative organization. It can take ten years to develop it, but only ten weeks to destroy it.

KEY POINTS

● Hierarchical organization and overt distinctions of status, especially if they breed deferential attitudes, are inimical to creative or innovative work. Keep structures as flat as possible, and relationships as informal as possible.

● In organizations towards the creative end of the spectrum it is essential that managers should be directors or leaders, otherwise they will lack credibility. Leadership implies leading by example, which usually means, in this context, having an output of creative work yourself.

● Water-tight compartments may prevent the ship sinking but they do not encourage intercourse among the ship's passengers. An innovative organization needs structures that permit — even encourage — cross-fertilization across the various boundaries at work.

● Because innovative organizations rely more upon shared ethos than adherence to written rules, special care has to be taken over recruitment. Intuition must pay a large part in the process, for academic qualifications or work record may not always be accurate predictions of creative potential. You need 'people-feel'.

● The ethos or climate of an innovative organization, however long established, is exceptionally vulnerable. Review any proposed changes in the light of what effect they will have upon the culture that has produced results.

> *The characteristic danger of great nations, like the Romans or the English, which have a long history of continuous creation, is that they at last fail from not comprehending the great institutions they have created.*
> *Walter Bagehot*

5. Case Study: Digital Equipment Corporation

An institution is the lengthened shadow of one man.

Emerson

Before discussing the second case study — Digital Equipment Corporation and its founder-leader Ken Olsen — I want to say a little more about bureaucracy. For it is clearly a potential enemy to innovation.

What kind of organization is outstandingly innovative? It is more easy to answer the question by identifying characteristics they do not have. They are not, for example, hierarchical or bureaucratic. As my conversation with Dr. Sydney Brenner, Director of the Laboratory of Molecular Biology at Cambridge, has already revealed, leaders of innovative organizations are constantly apprehensive about what they call 'bureaucracy'. But what is bureaucracy?

BUREAUCRACY VERSUS INNOVATION

The German sociologist Max Weber provided us with the first profile of a bureaucratic organization. In his writings bureaucracy simply describes a certain type of organization: the word did not have for him the pejorative sense that it has acquired for us. He summed up the distinctive characteristics of bureaucratic organizations as follows:

● authority is impersonal and formal;

● strong emphasis on functional specialization;

- a rule for every eventuality;

- strong emphasis on hierarchy and status;

- clearly laid down procedures (red tape);

- proliferation of paperwork;

- security of employment and advancement by seniority.

It is evident that an organization with this culture will tend to be rigid rather than flexible when it comes to responding to change. It is unlikely that it will encourage innovation; it may indeed actively seek to suppress it. 'Routine is the god of every social system,' wrote A. N. Whitehead. His words certainly apply to a true bureaucracy.

The word *bureaucracy* is a synthesis of the French word *burel* — a russet or coarse woollen cloth — and the Greek *kratos*, power. The russet woollen coats in question were worn by French clerks in the Civil Service. Therefore bureaucracy points to a system of government by officials, responsible only to their chiefs. Like all bad things the British tended to regard bureaucracy as a foreign invention. In the last century Thomas Carlyle, for example, numbered it among the 'continental nuisances'. Charles Kingsley wrote of plutocrats and bureaucrats as being 'the tyrants of the earth'. The French writer Balzac also disliked the new phenomenon: he called it 'a giant mechanism operated by pygmies.' As some wit put it, bureaucrats defend the *status quo* long after the *quo* has lost its *status*.

In mechanistic or machine-like organizations work is broken down into specialisms with somebody higher up being responsible for co-ordination. The duties, methods and boundaries of each part are prescribed in detail. Interaction is vertical: instructions come down and information flows up.

In more innovative organizations — those orientated to change and geared for creativity — there is much less definition of roles and responsibilities. Jobs are constantly being redefined in the light of changed circumstances. Each individual knows the overall purpose of the organization and the situational factors impacting upon it. They grasp the general strategic intentions of the leadership. People in such organizations interact as much laterally as vertically. Structure both reflects and facilitates that necessity by being more like a flat pyramid than a steep and multi-layered one. For top leaders are not approachable only through 'the appropriate channels'. There is ready access to them. Strategic leaders in turn spend much of their time talking to people at all levels.

These two types of organization — the bureaucratic or mechanistic one and the more flexible or organic one — are really two ends of a spectrum. Most organizations are blends of both the bureaucratic and the organic. The former principle stands for order and continuity; the latter spells freedom and change. Consequently organizations need to be both managed and led. At any one time, as we have already seen, the proper balance has to be struck between these two necessities.

There is no doubt that growth in size, together with the passage of years, increases the bureaucratic tendency. Insidiously and imperceptibly its ivy tentacles creep over the structure. Instead of the machine being well-oiled by commonsense and humming with energy it begins to slow down. More treacle is poured into the works. Paper proliferates. Even minor decisions are referred upwards. Systems regulate people. Systems regulate the systems. The senior managers become more remote and finally invisible. People begin to feel alienated. 'Things are not what they used to be here,' goes up the lament.

FIGHTING TO REMAIN ENTREPRENEURIAL

Where an entrepreneur retains the leadership of the growing organization he helped to create — by no means a universal phenomenon — he or she is well-placed to fight the onset of the bureaucratic culture. Ken Olsen of Digital Equipment Company (DEC) — described by *Fortune* in 1986 as 'arguably the most successful entrepreneur in the history of American business' — is one such leader. Since its birth over thirty years ago DEC has risen like a space rocket to become one of the world's larger computer manufacturers after IBM, with some 130,000 employees doing business in sixty five countries and manufacturing in eleven of them.

'I am always conscious of weaknesses in the company — places where the entrepreneurial spirit is lacking,' he told Tom Nash,

Assistant Editor of *Director*, in an interview published in August
1989. 'But I keep on correcting it. It's like raising children. You
don't ever get to the point where you succeed. You can always
improve.'

Olsen once described IBM as being like an old-style communist state — 'they knew nothing about the rest of the world, and
the world knew nothing about what went on inside.' He perceived the IBM approach to computing as being very different
from his own. 'Their approach is organized the way business is
organized,' he says. 'Everything is hierarchical. Everything goes
from the top down. They are evolving towards a more open
system, but they still have a tendency towards centralising. Their
networking is still concentrated on headquarters. Our approach
is more like a telephone network, where everyone can call everyone else. You have freedom and it is easy to make changes —
you just plug in like a telephone.'

According to Olsen, the memorable periods of DEC's development have been its various organizational changes. But in many
respects, he claims, managing a start-up, then a small fast-grow-
ing company and then a major multinational, presents essentially
the same challenge.

'Encouraging creativity and product development and the marketing of it is the same at all times,' he says. 'People need to be
trusted to set their goals and to have resources that will not be
taken away from them for no good reason. This is true when
you're small and when you're big.

'The one thing that destroys innovation is the risk of having
resources taken away, perhaps because someone more politically
capable has another project. In a small company it may be the
boss who changes his mind and in a large one it may be committees or controllers. But either way, it destroys motivation.

'The thing that gets more difficult as you get bigger is an
increase in the number of people who want to control everything.'

THE NECESSITY FOR RISK

The real point of Olsen's analogy between IBM and an old-
fashioned communist state emerges – now happily almost a thing
of the past – when he characterizes the communist system as

risk-averse. It 'doesn't work because they don't take risks. They don't give freedom to people to set goals and accomplish things,' he says.

'Yet we have an enormous tendency in companies to think that we have to control everything for efficiency. Control, control — people are always talking about control: don't allow duplications, don't allow risk taking. But this is what destroys creativity. Innovation means trying many things in the hope that some of them will succeed.'

DEC's first major organizational change took place in 1965 when it introduced a management structure that later became known as 'the matrix'. It won praise in Tom Peters and Robert Waterman's *In Search of Excellence*, although Olsen dislikes and does not use the term 'matrix'. Product groups were introduced each with its own manager, business plan and budget. Each product line manager had freedom to set his own goals and a budget that, once approved, could not be taken away. There were no barriers between product groups, so that a free exchange of knowledge could take place. Often described as a form of 'organized chaos', it allowed each manager to be genuinely entrepreneurial within the company — or 'intrapreneurial' in fashionable management jargon.

'It revolutionized the company,' says Olsen. 'We grew enormously because product line managers took responsibility for their own plans and made them work. The plan may not have been perfect, but they corrected it because it was theirs.'

But matrix organizations — where a person may belong to two or more teams at the same time — tend to be transitional. One or other of the arms of responsibility — geographical, product or business, professional specialism — tends to become the more dominant. Then something like a main hierarchical structure emerges again. But there is a difference, for it will be staffed by people who have 'matrix' written on their hearts. It is essential, in other words, to *think* in a matrix way in innovative organizations, even if the structure emphasizes one main line of accountability.

THE NEED FOR A LEADERSHIP TEAM

Leadership is also a critical issue in organizations that are
attempting to think and act in a matrix manner. One of Olsen's
problems, for example, was that he failed to develop a senior
leadership team who shared his philosophy. Therefore the heads
of product groups did not push down responsibility and decision-
making power as he had done. In this respect they mirrored
Olsen's own early reluctance to delegate, but he had learnt the
lesson and they had not.

'They did not see the need to pass on the freedom that I gave
to them. They were so much smarter than I was,' he told Tom
Nash with more than a touch of sarcasm. 'They were better
educated, spoke better, understood things better — even when
I couldn't control something of $14m without breaking it up,
they could control something of $1bn because they were so much
smarter.'

Olsen's enthusiasm for the matrix structure had all but with-
ered away by the early eighties and in 1983 he announced a new
management philosophy – one company working towards one
set of goals. Nevertheless, he still claims not to control the plans
and activities of his subordinates.

As a result of that reorganization virtually all the product line
managers left. 'I didn't fire them,' says Olsen. 'I asked them to
stay. But they were so confident, so experienced, so important,
working together was too humbling for them. They quit and
very few of them have done well.'

Olsen has never been afraid to get tough with individuals and
groups of managers who become obstructive, but his benevolence
still shows through. Getting tough is, he says, 'the hardest part
of being the boss because they're all good people with good
intentions.'

In keeping with Olsen's innovative philosophy is the firmly
established principle of 'single status' treatment of employees.
Despite his success and wealth Olsen remains remarkably unaf-
fected. 'There is nothing I won't do if it is important,' he says.
'There is nothing below my status.' There is, for example, no
hint of grandeur about his modestly furnished office in the con-
verted woollen mill in Maynard, Massachusetts, that has been
DEC's home since its birth. Although he shuns the trappings of
power the 'single status' principle is not taken to absurd

extremes. While all staff share the same dining rooms and car parks, Olsen has a reserved parking space for himself, on the grounds that he needs to be punctual at meetings.

'We make adjustments because none of these things is black and white,' he says. 'Honesty is the critical thing. If you want your employees to be honest, and you want your customers to trust you, you've got to be honest yourself.'

Not many companies achieve compound growth of twenty five per cent over two decades. No other high technology company has grown so fast for so long. The secret of DEC is its flexibility. When the market has changed the company has been able to change too. In other words, Ken Olsen and his team have built and sustained a great innovative organization. Can Olsen manage his departure, when the time comes, in such a way as to consolidate that achievement?

KEY POINTS

● It is fairly easy to identify the tell-tale symptoms of creeping bureaucracy. Although it is a legitimate and valuable form of organization for administrative purposes, bureaucracy is a hostile environment for new ideas and new ways of doing things.

● The innovative organization is the reverse image of bureaucracy: flat rather than pyramidical; decentralized decision-making and devolved responsibility; informal instead of formal; emphasis on lateral as well as vertical interaction; rules kept to a minimum; and positive about appropriate and properly calculated risks.

● As Ken Olsen points out, in innovative organizations managers have to curb their natural instinct to control everything. Control is an important leadership or management function, but it has to be exercised with skill and sensitivity. Thoroughbreds who know the course and enjoy jumping require a loose rein. Let the law of the situation do your controlling for you.

● When the market changes the innovative organization changes too.

● Without a leadership team at the top who value product
   quality, new ideas and innovation, and who constantly strug-
   gle to keep organizations moving towards these guiding stars,
   there will be no sustained and profitable growth.

                        What is honoured in a country will be culti-
                        vated there.

                                                           Plato

6. Real Commitment from the Top

Without real commitment from the top, real innovation will be defeated again and again by the policies, procedures, and rituals of almost any large organization.

Anon

The attitudes, personal qualities and skills of leaders in organizations stand out as a group of vitally important ingredients in innovation. Be they supervisors or first-line managers, middle managers or executive directors, the leaders of an enterprise can do a great deal to encourage creativity.

THE LEADER AS TEAMBUILDER

In both the above case studies — the Laboratory of Molecular Biology at Cambridge University and the Digital Equipment Corporation based in Massachusetts — the personality and example of the top leader was seen as a key factor in setting the direction and tone of an organization. What is required in a chief executive as a leader? The ability to build teamwork and create synergy comes high on the list.

Shortly after joining Chrysler, Lee Iacocca stumbled across a stunning revelation: 'Chrysler was like Italy in the 1860s — the company consisted of a cluster of little duchies, each one run by a prima donna,' he writes in *Iacocca: An autobiography*. 'It was a bunch of mini-empires, with nobody giving a damn about what anyone else was doing.' Iacocca knew he had to start immediately to build a team approach at every level. This was a key point in his outstanding leadership style.

Few managers have the talent of an Iacocca. Few do more than merely co-ordinate efforts. But the most effective leaders create a sense of *esprit de corps*, a team spirit that makes even the most arduous or the most humdrum work exciting. The synergy created supports and sustains the individuals in the group. At chief executive level, the successful leader's team will be a small group of executives and administrators who can think strategically with him or her, help to change the corporate culture towards greater teamwork, and devise the means of getting extraordinary results from the individuals who make up the workforce. Throughout the world, executives are waking up to the need for this kind of action-centred leadership as a means of realizing their company's potential.

Aware now of this new imperative to lead rather than merely manage, some adventurous chief executives have begun to take inventory of their leadership qualities and skills. For example, Theodore Brophy, the chairman and chief executive of the GTE Corporation in the United States, asked his ten direct subordinates to comment anonymously on his personal leadership. The purpose, he says, was to find out, among other things, 'the impact my style may be having upon them and their operations.'

These men and others have understood a basic truth: the chief executive who knows his strengths and weaknesses as a leader is likely to be far more effective than the one who remains blind to them. He may not be able to do much about his weaknesses, especially if he is over the age of fifty, but he is better equipped to compensate for them if he knows what they are. He also is on the road to humility — that priceless attitude of openness to life that can help a manager to absorb mistakes, failures or personal shortcomings.

The age of the autocratic boss, the one-man show, is over. The best organizations today tend to be led by a team. There is simply too much leadership required for any single person to provide it all. Well-managed companies today are guided by a team of leaders. The team itself needs a leader, however, and that is the core responsibility of the chief executive.

LEADER OR MANAGER — OR BOTH?

In responding to the challenge of innovation, *both* leadership *and* management skills are important, but the emphasis must fall on leadership. Therefore, leaders and potential leaders need an opportunity early on in their careers to explore the important new concept of leadership that is emerging — what it is, and how you can become more effective as a leader. The very definition of leadership is the first hurdle. Most of the world's business schools seem to be in a muddle over the issue. They are certainly not producing business leaders.

Abraham Zaleznik, a professor at the Harvard Business School, has been attempting to sort things out. Leaders, he says, are often dramatic and unpredictable in style. They tend to create a climate of change, sometimes not unlike chaos. They are 'often obsessed by their ideas, which appear visionary and consequently excite, stimulate and drive other people to work hard and create reality out of fantasy.' He considers Lee Iacocca such a leader.

Managers, Zaleznik continues, are typically hard-working, analytical, tolerant and fair-minded. They take much pride in perpetuating and improving upon the status quo, stemming from their strong sense of belonging to the organization. Such executives concentrate on process, whereas leaders focus on substance. Alfred Sloan, once boss of General motors, he regards as the classic manager.

Professor Zaleznik, then, seems to think that you are *either* a leader *or* a manager. But that is an over-simplification that obscures the truth. The best chief executives are both.

Sir Raymond Lygo, until recently head of British Aerospace and a former admiral in the Royal Navy, argues that the two concepts can be complementary if understood in these terms: 'Management is the art of organization, the art of organizing people and things to produce and achieve objectives. Leadership is the ability to inspire other men and women to achieve things much greater than they would have done if they were left to their own devices.'

Business and military organizations are fundamentally different in many ways, but this they share: both need leadership *and* management. So, I might add, do all organizations today that aspire to be innovative: universities, schools, hospitals, government departments, even churches. The highest levels should be occupied by those rare few who have both qualities.

GIVING DIRECTION

Organizations are unlikely to be innovative — to introduce change and make it effective — if they lack a sense of direction. If you are not facing the future and wanting to move forward, why change? But do you as a chief executive — or your chief executive — see the implications for your role?

Sir Alex Jarratt, as chairman of Reed International, posed the following question: 'Are you a helmsman or a navigator?' A helmsman is a 'hands-on' manager, a manager-leader who is guiding the day-to-day activities. A navigator has the capacity to stand back and plot the course of his ship.

I would argue that the chief executive must be both helmsman and navigator — as well as being captain. But he or she should not be more. I would not expect to find him in the engine room or peeling potatoes in the galley. The image of a ship under way at sea is especially apt. For the very word leader comes from *laed*, which meant in Old Norse the course or path of a ship at sea. The leader was the captain, who in Viking days was usually the steersman and navigator as well.

Like a ship, your business is sailing through difficult seas under the lowering skies of a difficult world economy. You have to contend with the forces of tide, wind and current. How good a helmsman are you? The art of helmsmanship, it is worth recalling, demands a subtle and sensitive exploration of how to extract the most power from wind and water. The best helmsmen are those who can find and hold that thin line of balance along which the elements seem to join in driving the boat forward. Is that not true for a business leader as well?

A helmsman, however, is only a tactician or an operator. A chief executive has to be a strategist too. That requires a vision of the future and the navigational skill to plot a course that will get your organization where it must be if that vision is to come true.

Let me hoist a warning at this point about the kind of corporate planning that flourished in the days when seas were calm and skies were blue. The drawback of these plans is obvious to us now. Senior managers, including the chief executive, often found these paper exercises irrelevant because they were not involved in the decisions and therefore not committed to getting results. One good result of the recession has been the closure or the drastic reduction of these mini-bureaucracies of corporate planning.

By a corporate plan I do not of course mean a detailed and watertight blueprint. Planning is good, but plans often are not. What you need is an agreed business philosophy, a comprehensive programme of clear objectives and definite policies.

To summarize, the first responsibility of leadership is *to achieve the common task*. In order to do that at his level the chief executive of any organization should have the following three characteristics:

● **The ability to think deeply.** Those who lead organizations in the right direction are going to have to possess practical intellect of high order. These thinking skills, such as analysing, imaginative and holistic thinking, intuition and judgement, are the foundation of a good decision-maker. As Sir Christopher Hogg, chairman of Courtaulds, has said: 'The one thing a chairman can do which no one else can is think. But the temptation is to start meddling instead.'

● **The ability to communicate.** As a chief executive, you should be a person with a message. All organizations tend to bow down to the god of routine. Your message is that we must look ahead and make pre-emptive changes.

● **The ability to make things happen.** That calls for a certain firmness of character. Be tough but fair. Toughness comes first, for that is necessary. You *have* to be tough, but toughness will only be acceptable if it is fair as well. You need other qualities as well — humour and infectious enthusiasm especially.

If you do not have a sense of direction, how can you lead? If a blind man leads a blind man, they will both fall into the ditch. To be a helmsman and a navigator for your organization you need the capacity to see ahead clearly, to communicate what you see and the qualities to ensure movement in that direction in a flexible way.

KEY POINTS

● Innovation calls for good leadership throughout an enterprise. Good leadership ought to stem from the chief executive. It is his or her prime responsibility to manage change. As the Roman author Publilius Syrus said, 'Anyone can hold the helm when the sea is calm.'

● To generate ideas and to see them transformed into profitable new products or services, to revitalize existing products and services with incremental improvements and to satisfy customers, demands high-performance teamwork. Teams look for leaders; leaders build teams.

● Without systems and proper controls sensibly applied, there can be no organization worthy of the name. It requires leadership *and* management to achieve productive order without sacrificing freedom and creativity.

● What matters most in organizations is energetic vision. Purpose is corporate energy, pulling you forwards and overcoming institutional inertia. Leaders are helmsmen and navigators, steering a course forwards through uncertainty and chaos.

● Strategic thinking and corporate planning both require creative thinking. If there is no innovation in the boardroom why should there be any on the shopfloor?

> *Changing things is central to leadership.*
> *Changing them before anyone else is creative-*
> *ness.*
>
> *Anon*

7. How To Motivate The Creative Individual

The best of men are but men at their best.
English proverb

As a manager you need to understand how creative or innovative individuals think and what they want. For innovation will not happen unless the men and women who work with you are motivated. They must WANT to innovate.

According to the Fifty-Fifty Rule (see my *Understanding Motivation*), fifty percent of motivation lies within us in the shape of our response to inner needs, drives and values. The other fifty percent depends on our environment, especially the leadership that we encounter within it. As a corollary of that rule, it is important first to get your selection procedures right. Choose people who have the seeds of the future within them.

SELECTING CREATIVE PEOPLE

When Dr David Livingstone was working in Africa, a group of friends wrote: 'We would like to send other men to you. Have you found a good road into your area yet?'

According to a member of his family, Dr Livingstone sent this message in reply: 'If you have men who will only come if they know there is a good road, I don't want them. I want men who will come if there is no road at all.'

The first step in any form of team building is to choose the right people. That is a vital principle to bear in mind if you wish to encourage innovation — and sustain it. Like Dr Livingstone, in his inimitable way, you should develop an eye for the more adventurous and more independently-minded person. As Sam

Goldwyn put it, 'I don't want any yes-men around me. I want everyone to tell the truth even if it costs them their jobs!'

When it comes to innovation there has to be a premium on youth. Young people tend to be more future-orientated. After all, most of their life will be spent in the future. Moreover, the fact that young people lack experience (which could almost be defined as the knowledge of what does not work) inclines them to be ready to experiment. They have less mental luggage in the form of preconceptions or assumptions. The older we grow in years the more cautious and the more conservative we tend to become. 'Men of age object too much, consult too long, adventure too little, repent too soon,' wrote Francis Bacon in a pithy summary of what comes with over-maturity. You can see why Napoleon once mused that the art of government was not to let people grow old in their jobs.

Any innovative organization must therefore have a bias towards attracting intelligent and creative young people. Of course intellectual qualities are not enough, for industry needs *doers* — people who can make things happen — rather than *thinkers* as such. There are plenty of good ideas around. The real issue is whether or not you have the people in your team or organization who are willing to put new ideas to work, in other words, to innovate. 'Give me the young man,' said Robert Louis Stevenson, 'who has brains enough to make a fool of himself.'

How will you recognize creativity? It is rather like height, weight and strength. We vary considerably in these dimensions, but all of us have some height, some weight and some strength. Thus there is a certain amount of potential for creative thinking in all of us, but some people are clearly more creative than others. Your organization needs its fair share of this creative talent.

You can usually identify some general characteristics. Creative people tend to be more open and flexible than their less creative neighbours. They bring a freshness of mind to problems. They have usually exhibited the courage to be different and to think for themselves. They are comparatively more self-motivated and are often addicted to their work. Research has both illuminated and added to this brief list. Here is an expanded list of twelve characteristics to look for in studying references, biographical data or during interviews.

TWELVE CHARACTERISTICS OF INNOVATORS

Creative or innovative people can usually be recognized by having a pattern of characteristics represented in the list below. Such people do not make natural organizational men and women, and so your organization needs a certain psychological maturity to recruit them in the first place. Creative people can make uncomfortable companions, but can you do without them? Here are the characteristics to look for:

● Superior general intelligence. That includes analytical powers, as well as the ability to store and recall information.

● A high degree of autonomy, self-sufficiency and self-direction.

● Relatively little talkativeness or gregariousness. Creative thinkers tend to be ambivert: a balance of introvert and extrovert. If anything they tend towards introversion, although they need contacts with stimulating colleagues.

● Marked independence of judgement. They are resilient in the teeth of group pressures towards conformity in thinking. They see things as others do, but also as they do not.

● They often express part-truths vividly. It is their way of drawing attention to the unobserved or unrecognized. They may sound unreasonable. But remember George Bernard Shaw's provocative comment: 'The reasonable man adapts himself to the world: the unreasonable one persists in trying to adapt the world to himself. Therefore all progress depends on the unreasonable man.'

● A broad range of interests.

● A special interest or motivation in the kind of 'wagering' which involves pitting oneself against problems or opportunities in which one's own effort can be the deciding factor. 'There is no greater joy in life,' said the inventor Sir Barnes Wallis, 'than first proving that a thing is impossible and then showing how it can be done.'

● Sustained curiosity and powers of observation. Often they are good listeners.

● Dedication and commitment to hard work.

● A truly creative individual lives closer to his or her purposeful unconscious mind than other people. He or she listens to the truth from within, in the form of intuitions. They inhabit more the world of imagination, reverie and fantasy.

● They are able to hold many ideas — often apparently contradictory ones — together in creative tension, without reaching for premature resolution of ambiguity. Hence they can sometimes reach a richer synthesis.

From the analysis it follows that if you do recruit or select people with above-average creative ability for your team or organization you will find that they tend to be looking for certain compatible characteristics in you and your organization. Selection is — or ought to be — a two-way process. Before you take on creative people you should check whether or not you have the environment (including leadership) in which their talents will flourish. It is not much good to hire people who are only going to become frustrated. What are their expectations?

EXPECTATIONS OF CREATIVE PEOPLE

Research has some clear messages on this score. It has identified the most important environmental factors in stimulating or encouraging creativity. In order of importance they are as follows:

● *Recognition and appreciation*
Because the results of creative work are often postponed for a long time (many geniuses in history received no recognition in their lifetimes), creative people stand in special need of encouragement and appreciation. The recognition of the value or worth of their contribution is especially important to them, particularly if it comes from those whose opinions they respect. For example, winning a Nobel prize means a great deal to a research scientist.

Scientists in particular are often competitive and achievement-orientated. Recognition matters much more to them than money, though the latter is not insignificant on the scale of reward.

Lewis Lehr highlights the importance in 3M of giving proper recognition:

> 'One or two dozen times a year some new 3M project reaches the level of $2 million in profitable sales. You might think that drop wouldn't get much attention in an $8 billion ocean. But it does. Lights flash, bells ring, and cameras are called out to honour the team responsible for such an achievement. We see in these fledgling projects the future of 3M. We also have recognition programmes for international business successes, for purely technical achievements, and for outstanding work in virtually every discipline within the company.
>
> 'These awards rarely take the form of cash bonuses or trips to Hawaii. We have found that, especially for technical people, few things are more important than simply being recognized by one's peers for good work. Recognition is a powerful incentive for innovation.'

● *Freedom to work in areas of greatest interest*

While the predominantly analytical person concentrates and focusses down, the creative person wanders in every possible or feasible direction. Freedom to move is the necessary condition of creative work. A creative person tends to be most effective if allowed to choose the area of work, and the problems or opportunities within that area, which arouse deep interest.

Clearly within an innovative organization this freedom has to be bounded by its definition of general purpose and by the consequent parameters of its broad strategies. The Laboratory for Molecular Biology at Cambridge, for instance, made it clear to potential research staff that it was not in the business of brain research. But if the mission statement of the organization is properly focussed — the horizon between the general, far away and vague on the one hand, and the more specific and more proximate on the other — then there will be a wide area for exploration.

Successful innovative companies such as 3M lean over backwards to give individuals as much freedom as possible. Lewis Lehr again:

'Advice on rearing creative youngsters states that you *don't* provide
children with colouring books and then warn them to stay inside
the lines of the drawings. For management to expect innovators
to stay inside the lines is a paradox. Such inhibiting boundaries
may be job descriptions, detailed instructions on how to do something, or any restrictive language. Long ago we learned that if you
place too many fences around people, they can easily become a
pasture of sheep. And how many patents are assigned to sheep?'

In 3M the top management encourages the technical staff to
spend up to fifteen per cent of their time on projects of their
own choosing. In other words, the company *guarantees time* for
people to work on pet ideas. They can at least start work on
something without waiting for management approval.

Sensible companies also establish a career path for creative
individuals separate from the management ladder, a corporate
path that allows them to go on doing what they do best as
individual contributors. Some will want to become manager-
leaders, but others will prefer the freedom of remaining individual contributors. For the latter financial remuneration and pro-
motion can be linked directly to successful innovation. Beyond
these rewards they receive the prize of earned freedom to work
on whatever interests them. IBM's corporate fellows, for
instance, are given freedom for a time to roam the company and
work on whatever project interests them. Innovative organizations can also, of course, draw upon the contributions of creative
thinkers who are not their full-time employees and therefore
have a much greater freedom to pursue their own interests.

● *Contacts with stimulating colleagues*
'Two heads are better than one,' says the ancient Greek proverb.
Creative people need conversation with colleagues in order to
think, not merely for social intercourse. In the social sense they
may even be inclined to be 'loners', but they cannot intellectually
be 'loners' all the time. Organizational structure should facilitate
these formal and informal interactions. Buildings, especially the
position and character of rooms where people congregate for
coffee, tea or meals, play an important part. Random meetings
with colleagues and visitors in such meeting places may spark
off new ideas or suggest new avenues of thought.

● *Encouragement to take risks*

To quote Sydney Brenner's words again, 'Innovation is a gamble.' If you have never worked on the edge of failure, you will not have worked on the edge of real success. Creative people respond well to an organization which encourages them to take calculated risks.

* * *

These above environmental conditions become motivational in conjunction with the inner interests and drives of creative individuals. The ensuing chemistry — the interaction of creative individual and innovative group or organization — produces the new goods and services. The resultant social and economic advances, together with an invisible movement of the human spirit, are what we collectively call PROGRESS.

There are other less important but still significant factors in the environment which matter to the creative individual, such as its tolerance of a degree of nonconformity or idiosyncrasy, the opportunity to work alone as opposed to being always as member of a group, and the level of financial reward. But the important lesson for organizations is to look after the major expectations first. The minor ones can be the subject of negotiation.

CREATIVE LEADERSHIP

Apart from being able to provide general direction and to perform the necessary leadership functions — defining objectives, planning, controlling, supporting, reviewing — to meet the three overlapping areas of task, team and individual needs, leaders who encourage creativity have some distinctive characteristics. You may like to consider adopting them if they are not already present in your approach. The useful guidelines include:

● *A Willingness to Accept Risk*

The potential downside of freedom given to a colleague or team, as we have seen, includes mistakes, failures or financial loss. As delegation should not mean abdication, so you as the leader may well have been a party to the risk. You may at least have understood the consequences of things not going as intended or planned. You have to be willing to accept an element of risk. For without freedom there would be no mistakes. But to eliminate freedom is the biggest mistake of all. For freedom alone breeds innovation and entrepreneurial success. Mistakes are a by-product of progress. Learn from them, but do not dwell on them.

● An Ability to Work with Half-Baked Ideas

Ideas seldom leap into the world fully-formed and ready to go. They are more like new-born babies, struggling and gasping for life. Leaders who facilitate team creativity demonstrate by example the value of listening to half-developed ideas and building upon them if they have merit. They hesitate before dismissing an ill-formed idea or an imperfect proposal, for it may contain the germ of something really useful. It follows that team creativity in groups and organizations calls for *listening* leaders.

● A Willingness to Bend Rules

Rules and systems have their place, but they can obstruct the process of innovation dreadfully. A leader, as a member of the management team, should respect rules and procedures but he or she should not *think* like a bureaucrat. Sometimes creative dyslexia — the inability to read rules — is a strength rather than a weakness. Rules can sometimes be stretched where they cannot be broken. Otherwise you end up by being bogged down in organizational treacle — or, as Charles Dickens said, 'Skewered through and through with office-pens and bound hand-and-foot with red tape.' Remember that Nelson once put his telescope to his blind eye. Having a blind eye can be a strength on occasion, not a weakness.

● An Ability to Respond Quickly

On the new-baby analogy, some new ideas or projects need sustenance quickly if they are going to survive. Leaders who induce creativity should have a flair for spotting potential winners. But that is not enough. The innovative organization must have leaders who are able to commit resources and not have to defer everything to committees or upwards to Higher Authority. To be able to allocate or obtain small resources now may be far better than being able to summon mighty resources in a year's time when it is too late. That is why some organizations appoint 'project sponsors' — senior managers who are able to secure resources at a high level quickly for promising ideas.

● *Personal Enthusiasm*

Only leaders who are highly motivated themselves will motivate others. Enthusiasm is contagious. Moreover, enthusiastic leaders and colleagues tend to be intellectually stimulating ones. 'Man never rises to great truths without enthusiasm,' wrote Vauvenargues. Innovation usually deals in small truths or incremental improvements, but the same principle holds good.

KEY POINTS

● A house is made up of individual bricks. The quality of an innovative organization depends ultimately and largely upon the quality of the people you employ. Machines do not have new ideas. Computers cannot create. Money alone cannot create a satisfied customer.

● Look out for the twelve characteristics — or clusters of characteristics — which mark creative people. Ensure that many of those you appoint have some of these characteristics.

● There will always be a tension between the needs of the individual and the needs of the common task and the needs of the group or organization. If you have good leadership this tension should be a creative one. Under bad management, however, it degenerates into conflict.

● Creative thinkers and innovative doers will not stay with you unless you give them recognition. For recognition and appreciation come top of the list of expectations that creative people bring with them to work.

● Creative leadership means the kind of leadership that encourages, stimulates and guides the process of innovation from beginning to end. The challenge of innovation is largely the challenge of leading creative people.

*What a man dislikes in his superiors, let him
not display in his treatment of his inferiors.*
                                    Tsang Sin

8. Team Creativity

Many ideas grow better when transplanted into another mind than in the one where they sprang up.

Oliver Wendell Holmes

A new idea almost invariably comes from an individual. But it takes a team to turn it into something really useful.

From this principle, as stated thus, it would be easy to dichotomize the process. The individual who has the new idea is being *creative*, you might say, while the group or organization that develops it is being *innovative*. But this would be an oversimplification. What the individual usually comes up with is a half-formed idea. That is often, incidentally, the result of preliminary discussion with colleagues. Then that half-baked idea is creatively developed by one or more others working like a team. The whole process is best called TEAM CREATIVITY.

The Japanese economy has been transformed by the practical application of that concept. As individuals the Japanese are not noted for their creativity. Indeed Japanese culture, especially its educational system, has traditionally played down individuality. 'If a nail stands up, it will be hammered down,' declares a Japanese proverb bluntly. That is not a spirit which develops much creativity in individuals. But in groups the Japanese have shown themselves to be remarkably innovative. In the West we may have been over-emphasizing the role of the individual in the context of creativity. If you look closely at creative thinking — even apparently solitary creators like authors, inventors or artists — there is a considerable input from others before and after the emergence of a seminal idea. Being human and anxious for personal recognition, individuals often over-emphasize their own parts. And Western society conspires by recognizing and rewarding individuals rather than teams for creative work.

BUILDING ON IDEAS

How can team creativity be promoted in a group or an organization? One solution, which will be discussed in the following
chapter, is to introduce a new system of groups, like the
Japanese-inspired Quality Circles. If I may anticipate the argument, however, such special groups only flourish under a management which is *already* orientated towards team creativity.

The essence of the matter lies in attitudes. It is a question of
moving a group or organization away from the position where
the natural response to a half-baked idea is a negative or critical
one. The expression of a more positive attitude is the observed
willingness to BUILD ON IDEAS.

Let us visualize two meetings. In Group A a number of suggestions are made or ideas put forward for consideration. These
ideas are not picked up or developed by anyone else. They
disappear into the pond with a 'plop'. Some of these plops might,
of course, have the seeds within them of new ideas. The meeting
of Group A looks like this:

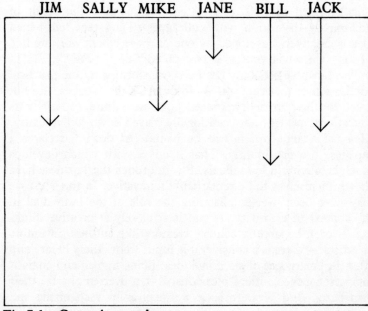

Fig 7.1   *Group A at work*

The different lengths of lines represents the extent of contribution. Bill, for example, developed his ideas at some length, whereas Jane made one short contribution which was hardly heard above the hubbub of conversation. The listening skills were low in Group A. Indeed they were confined to waiting until other people had stopped speaking so that each could have his or her turn to talk. More often than not, two or three people were speaking at the same time.

You will notice that Group B is composed of the same individuals as Group A. But they are now acting differently. Instead of waiting for their turn to speak they are listening for ideas. When they see an idea they do not shoot it down. If they perceive some merit in it they will build on it. On the left hand side of the diagram Jim, for example, proposes a certain solution. Sally develops the idea further. Jack then works on it. What he says inspires Sally who comes back with some further modifications and the team realizes that it has a workable idea.

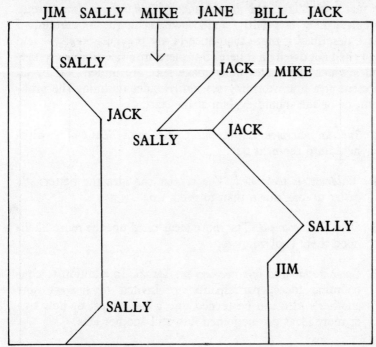

Fig. 7.2   *Group B at work*

Further to the right, Jack at first develops an idea of Jane's in one direction. Then he sees a link with an idea originated by Bill (which Mike has already made into a better one). Sally and Jim then work on the resultant new idea, bringing it to fruition.

The model is not unlike an aerial photograph of a game of football, with 'touch-down' being scored at the bottom end. Group A, you recall, scored no touch-downs. By working as a team, however, in their new colours as Group B, they became remarkably successful.

The secret is changing attitudes and moving from the negative or critical mode of thinking into the positive or constructive one. As Winston Churchill said at one cabinet meeting, in some exasperation at his timorous colleagues, 'Every fool can see what is wrong. See what is good in it!'

BRAINSTORMING

One of the great contributions of brainstorming as a technique is that it highlights this importance of *building on ideas*. Group brainstorming is a fairly well-known technique — certainly I have described it more than once in my previous books — and so I shall not dwell on it here. But there are a few simple ground-rules which the leader must make sure are understood by all present at a brainstorming session. Besides outlining the problem, he or she should explain at the start:

● *Judicial judgement is ruled out.* Criticism of ideas will be withheld until the next day.

● *'Wildness' is welcomed.* The crazier the idea the better; it's easier to tone down than to think up.

● *Quantity is wanted.* The more ideas piled up, the more likelihood there is of winners.

● *Combination and improvement are sought.* In addition to contributing ideas, participants are invited to suggest how another's idea can be turned into a *better* idea; or how two or more ideas can be joined into still another idea.

These are the guidelines. A leader should put them into his

or her own words because a brainstorm session should always be kept informal. Here's how one leader interpreted the first principle to one of his groups:

'If you try to get hot and cold water out of the same tap at the same time,' he said, 'you will get only tepid water. And if you try to criticize *and* create at the same time, you can't turn on either *cold* enough criticism or *hot* enough ideas. So let's stick solely to *ideas* — let's cut out *all* criticism during this session.'

A few incurable critics may still ignore the guidelines and belittle what others have suggested. Such transgressions should be gently warned against, and — if persistent — firmly checked. For the *spirit* of a brainstorm session can make or break it. Self-encouragement and mutual encouragement are both needed. The kind of criticism which cramps imagination, however, breeds discouragement.

There are few people who have participated in brainstorm-sessions who have not experienced 'chain-reaction': when minds are really warmed up, and a spark from one mind will light up a lot of ideas in others like a string of fire-crackers. Association of ideas comes into play, so that an idea put into words stirs your imagination towards another idea, while at the same time it stimulates associative connections in other people's minds, often at a subconscious level.

Putting ideas into words, however ill-formed, is the vital step in brainstorming. As the seventeenth century poet Edward Young wrote, 'Thoughts shut up want air, and spoil like bales unopen'd to the sky.'

Both as an educational method and as an informal technique for generating ideas, brainstorming has proved its worth since Alex Osborn first introduced it in *Applied Imagination* (1952). It was an early pointer to the much wider concept of team creativity.

TEAM CREATIVITY IN ACTION

The invention of Scotch Tape in 1930 is a highlight in the story of 3M, the Minnesota corporation that grew from being a maker of mediocre sandpaper into an international conglomerate:

The salesmen who visited the auto plants noticed that workers painting new two-toned cars were having trouble keeping the colours from running together. Richard G. Drew, a young 3M lab technician, came up with the answer: masking tape, the company's first tape. In 1930, six years after Du Pont introduced cellophane, Drew figured out how to put adhesive on it, and Scotch Tape was born, initially for industrial packaging. It didn't really begin to roll until another imaginative 3M hero, John Borden, a sales manager, created a dispenser with a built-in blade.

You can see that members of this company had learned to build on one another's ideas. The process of innovation is largely incremental. It requires the efforts and contributions of a team if an idea is to be brought successfully to the marketplace. Rarely is an idea marketable as it is conceived in someone's mind. It generally takes some research, much refining and a lot of hard work — sometimes over years — before it comes into common usage.

By hindsight, in the clear light of success or failure, it seems obvious what were the good ideas and what were the less feasible ones. In the early stages, however, the distinction is not so apparent. 'The sublime and the ridiculous are often so nearly related,' wrote Thomas Paine, 'that it is difficult to class them separately. One step above the sublime makes the ridiculous, and one step above the ridiculous makes the sublime again.'

The ability to suspend judgement for a time — both as an individual thinker and as a team member — is important. The ability, too, to build on other people's ideas, improving or combining them, is essential. But these two abilities do not exhaust the repertoire of skills required in a member of a truly innovative organization. The ability to criticize in an acceptable and diplomatic manner — in the right way, at the right time and in the right place — has also to be developed.

Here team creativity transcends brainstorming which, by definition, eliminates criticism. It is really no more than a snapshot of one phase of creative teamwork. Analysing and evaluating are equally necessary phases in the shared mental process. Again, as in the case of synthesizing and imagining, when it comes to analysing and evaluating there is a musical relationship between the individual thinker and the group. The 'solo' thinker may suggest themes developed by a section of the orchestra; another soloist may take forwards a refrain identified by the players as a whole.

TEAM CREATIVITY AND ORGANIZATION

Looking at the organization as a whole, the team creativity principle stresses that everyone has a contribution to make to the innovative process. It is as if there is a continual *conversation* going on within the organization about its products and services, about its structures and about its environment. It ought to be a *learning* conversation, the principal means by which the organization thinks in the sense of trying to teach itself what it should be and do. In this respect an innovative organization will resemble a true university.

In *The Voice of Liberal Learning: Michael Oakeshott on Education* (edited by Timothy Fuller, Yale University Press, 1989), the distinguished political philosopher offers a lucid summary of what a real university is actually about. His words apply also to any innovative organization:

'The pursuit of learning is not a race in which the competitors jockey for the best place, it is not even an argument or a symposium; it is a conversation. And the peculiar virtue of a university (as a place of many studies) is to exhibit it in this character, each study appearing as a voice whose tone is neither tyrannous nor plangent, but humble and conversable. A conversation does not need a chairman, it has no predetermined course, we do not ask what it is "for", and we do not judge its excellence by its conclusion; it has no conclusion, but is always put by for another day. Its integration is not superimposed but springs from the quality of the voices which speak, and its value lies in the relics it leaves behind in the minds of those who participate . . .

'A university will have ceased to exist when its learning has degenerated into what is now called research, when its teaching has become mere instruction and occupies the whole of an undergraduate's time, and when those who came to be taught come, not in search of their intellectual fortune but with a vitality so unroused or so exhausted that they wish only to be provided with a serviceable moral and intellectual outfit; when they come with no understanding of the manners of conversation but desire only a qualification for earning a living or a certificate to let them in on the exploitation of the world.'

Team creativity cannot be organized, but there are structures which encourage it, providing you have selected the right participants. The ethos of a group or organization is obviously important. The right climate will encourage people to express ideas, however half-formed. Members are able to discipline themselves in order to suspend judgement. They listen for ideas. They build and improve on one another's contributions. In other words, the *conversation* in that organization is positive, confident but realistic, and essentially constructive. Criticism is necessary, too, because it is a vital ingredient in effective thinking. How is it to be done?

HOW TO CRITICIZE OTHER PEOPLE'S IDEAS

'A new idea is delicate,' said Charles Brower. 'It can be killed by a sneer or a yawn; it can be stabbed to death by a quip and worried to death by a frown on the right man's brow.'

The management of criticism is almost as important as the management of innovation. Criticism has to be done. For expensive mistakes may occur, leading organizations up blind and profitless alleys, if ideas are not evaluated rigorously at the right time. Henry Ford used to content himself with three questions:

> IS IT NEEDED?
> IS IT PRACTICAL?
> IS IT COMMERCIAL?

These questions do have to be pressed home hard in commercial and industrial organizations. But they should not be applied prematurely in the creative process. Sometimes ideas have to evolve quite far before any practical and commercial use becomes apparent. But tested they must be by others at various stages of their life history. The good ones are those which can jump the hurdles of criticism.

Testing or criticizing other people's new ideas — and being on the receiving end of that treatment — is often not a pleasant process. It can be downright demoralizing to the receiver. We have to learn what Michael Oakeshott called 'the manners of conversation'. In the context of criticism, that means learning to express our views with tact and diplomacy.

Francis Crick, co-discoverer with James Watson of the double helix, describes in his biography *What Mad Pursuit: A Personal View of Scientific Discovery* (1988), two valuable lessons about criticism. He had joined the group studying molecular biology in the Cavendish Laboratory at Cambridge, which formed the nucleus later for the independent Laboratory for Molecular Biology. The group was under the general supervision of Sir Lawrence Bragg, a Nobel laureate for his work on X-ray crystallography.

At this time Crick was over thirty, with no research record to speak about. But he told the group that they were all wasting their time, for, according to his analyses, almost all the methods they were pursuing had no chance of success. He read them a paper — only his second research paper — entitled 'What Mad Pursuit!' — a quotation from Keats' *Ode on a Grecian Urn*. He continues:

'Bragg was furious. Here was this newcomer telling experienced X-ray crystallographers, including Bragg himself, who had founded the subject and been in the forefront of it for almost forty years, that what they were doing was most unlikely to lead to any useful result. The fact that I clearly understood the theory of the subject and indeed was apt to be unduly loquacious about it did not help. A little later I was sitting behind Bragg, just before the start of a lecture, and voicing to my neighbour my usual criticism of the subject in a rather derisive manner. Bragg turned around to speak to me over his shoulder. "Crick," he said, "you're rocking the boat."

'There was some justification for his annoyance. A group of people engaged in a difficult and somewhat uncertain undertaking are not helped by persistent negative criticism from one of their number. It destroys the mood of confidence necessary to carry through such a hazardous enterprise to a successful conclusion. But equally it is useless to persist in a course of action that is bound to fail, especially if an alternative method exists. As it has turned out, I was completely correct in all my criticisms with one exception. I underestimated the usefulness of studying simple, repeating, artificial peptides (distantly related to proteins), which before long was to give some useful information, but I was quite correct in predicting that only the isomorphous replacement method could give us the detailed structure of a protein.

'I was still, at this time, a beginning graduate student. By giving my colleagues a very necessary jolt I had deflected their attention in the right direction. In later years few people remembered this or appreciated my contribution except Bernal, who referred to it more than once. Of course in the long run my point of view was bound to emerge. All I did was to help create an atmosphere in which it happened a little sooner. I never wrote up my critique, though my notes for the talk survived for a few years. The main result as far as I was concerned was that Bragg came to regard me as a nuisance who didn't get on with experiments and talked too much and in too critical a manner. Fortunately he changed his mind later on.'

Crick points us here to one aspect of the truth about criticism. Sometimes an individual needs to be courageous in challenging accepted views, and to persist in criticism despite group pressures to conform. Such criticism may be voiced in vivid language in order that it may penetrate the thick hides of fixed ideas and win a hearing for itself. It may be consciously rejected, Crick notes, but it is yet to have influence at a subliminal level on the corporate unconscious mind of the group, perhaps even altering its direction of thought.

That was not, however, the only lesson about criticism that Crick learnt:

'I received another lesson when Perutz described his results to a small group of X-ray crystallographers from different parts of Britain assembled in the Cavendish. After his presentation, Bernal rose to comment on it. I regarded Bernal as a genius. For some reason I had acquired the idea that all geniuses behaved badly. I was therefore surprised to hear him praise Perutz in the most genial way for his courage in undertaking such a difficult and, at that time, unprecedented task and for his thoroughness and persistence in carrying it through. Only then did Bernal venture to express, in the nicest possible way, some reservations he had about the Patterson method and this example of it in particular. I learned that if you have something critical to say about a piece of scientific work, it is better to say it firmly but nicely and to preface it with praise of any good aspects of it. I only wish I had always stuck to this useful rule. Unfortunately I have sometimes been carried away by my impatience and expressed myself too briskly and in too devastating a manner.'

Being able to operate effectively in a situation that calls for team creativity does invite you to develop the skill of giving criticism in a constructive way and with good manners. It is obviously easier to accept criticism of one's ideas or work if it is offered in the same positive spirit and delivered with the same tact and diplomacy. But avoid dismissing criticism which has none of these hallmarks.

KEY POINTS

● Team creativity points to the fact that more than one person is involved in any significant act of creative thinking. This is even more apparent when it comes to innovation. To develop a product or service from an idea, however mature, self-evidently requires creative teamwork.

● At the core of team creativity is the capacity to build upon or improve other people's ideas, and to subject your own ideas to the same process. 'The typical eye sees the ten per cent bad of an idea,' writes Charles F. Kettering, 'and overlooks the ninety per cent good.'

● Building on ideas sounds a simple recipe, and so it is. But it presupposes a positive and constructive ethos, mutual encouragement, and the ability to listen.

● Although it may be focussed in particular meetings or even in departments, such as research and development, team creativity should embrace the whole organization. It should be a basic theme in the endless conversation of any organization that seeks to be innovative.

● The brainstorming technique illustrates the benefit of separating imaginative thinking from critical thinking. But ideas do have to be subjected to rigorous evaluation at some stage or other. To be able to give criticism effectively, and to receive it, is an art that has to be learnt.

> *He that wrestles with us strengthens our nerves and sharpens our skill. Our antagonist is our helper.*
>
> *Edmund Burke*

9. Harvesting Ideas

*The creative act thrives in an environment of
mutual stimulation, feedback and constructive
criticism — in a community of creativity.*
                              William T. Brady

Each person that works with you has about 10,000 million brain-cells. Each of those cells can link up with about 10,000 of its neighbours, giving some one plus eight hundred noughts of possible combinations. He or she has more braincells than there are people on the face of the earth. Your challenge as a leader is to elicit the new ideas and fresh thinking which is potentially there in those who work with you. 'In the coldest flint there is a hot fire.'

One way of doing so is to introduce what could be called innovative systems, notably Suggestion Schemes and Quality Circles, which are designed to encourage and harvest ideas at work.

Managers who are not leaders tend to believe that *all* problems can be solved by introducing a system. But systems are usually only half the solution. The other half is the people running them and the people participating in them. That spells out the need for leadership at all levels, together with a sound recruitment policy coupled with a comprehensive training programme. There is no such thing as instant innovation.

SUGGESTION SCHEMES

In 1857 the Chance Brothers of Smethwick, surprised when their workers suggested ways of improving production and saving on materials, hit upon the idea of putting a wooden box where such ideas could be posted. The scheme proved to be of immense

worth to the firm and to the workers. It was the world's first
Suggestion Scheme.

Suggestion Schemes were not widely adopted, however, until
this century. The Great Western Railway introduced one in 1913,
and British Rail has perpetuated the tradition.

The kind of idea which won awards from British Rail in the 1980s
was furnished by a fitter who pointed out that there would be
considerable saving if hydraulic pan jacks were re-sleeved with
stainless steel liners. His reward was £500. Another employee
suggested an improved design for shelves in the attendants' compartments in the new Mark III sleeping cars. He received £300.
But for enthusiasm in offering suggestions a railway employee with
sixty years' service would be hard to beat. During his working life
he offered no less than 30,800 ideas, thus earning himself a place
in the Guinness Book of Records, if they earned him nothing else.

In America the United States Navy had a fully-fledged Suggestion Scheme in operation in 1918, but the American companies
that followed suit tended to abandon the practice in the years of
peace. The Second World War brought a revival, with some six
thousand schemes in operation paying out an estimated five
billion dollars. The War Department alone received 20,069 ideas
from its employees in 18 months, and awarded $44 million in
prizes.

'The enthusiastic support of top-management is essential,' con-
cluded the American writer Alex Osborn in a survey of Suggestion Schemes in 1948. He ridiculed those managers who merely
affixed a wooden box for suggestions in the work place and sat
back to await a few million-dollar ideas.

How do you increase the yield and quality of ideas? Osborn
underlined the importance of focus. It is not enough to take a
general theme each year, such as customer service or sales. Ask
some pointed questions. Give people a fairly specific direction
for their thinking. For, as Osborn said, 'Our imaginations must
have bones to gnaw upon.'

A management-leadership team that is *eager* for innovation —
one which *expects* ideas and which is *determined* to generate
them — is much more likely to enjoy a successful and profitable
Suggestion Scheme. That is the first requirement. The second
essential is simplicity. Keep your Suggestion Scheme as simple

as possible. The more complicated and bureaucratic it becomes, the less effective it will be.

A quick response to new ideas or suggestions is also essential. Knowledge of results is always motivating. Conversely, not knowing what has happened to your bright idea for months on end is extremely demotivating and demoralizing. The system must be such that participants know fairly soon if the organization is saying yes, no or wait.

If the answer is no it is important to explain why in some detail. That requires either a personal letter or, more preferably, a short meeting. Research suggests that people are not demotivated if their idea is rejected, providing the reasons for doing so are set out clearly and convincingly. Needless to add, work people stand in as much need of tact and diplomacy when their ideas are being rejected as scientists, managers or professional people.

'Pride is really the first thing that matters; the money comes second. To be picked out of a corporation like British Airways is really something.' So said Michael Rowlerson, winner of a national competition for suggestions in Britain, when asked about the £5000 he received from British Airways for suggesting how to remove corrosion from the inside of undercarriage struts. To repeat the point, the general consensus is that money is not the prime motivator when it comes to generating new ideas: recognition and sense of achievement are way ahead of it. But that should not prevent companies from giving more realistic monetary prizes both as signs of recognition and also as incentives to others.

Suggestion Schemes, to enjoy success, need to be marketed internally. Special events, publicity, newsletters and local newspaper or radio, together with a lively and compelling promotional booklet, are all ingredients in keeping the system alive and functioning well. Never expect any system to go on working without maintenance, revision and re-inspiration.

Granted these ingredients, Suggestion Schemes are a most valuable system for harvesting innovative ideas. At Adams Foods, for example, one employee, originally a butter packer, has moved into design engineering as a result of a suggestion he made to redesign a machine. He was given a week off with a design engineer to put his suggestion into practice and the redesign has saved the company £90,000 in the last eight years.

The Rover Group claimed that it had saved over £3 million as a result of the 1,400 suggestions adopted in 1988. The accumulated savings over four years amount to nearly £40 million and a third of the workforce regularly offers new ideas to save the business money and smooth production. Ideas can range from how to cut down on paper clips to technical changes — such as the proposal from two workers, which earned them £5,000. They suggested changing the electrical systems which power the plant's fork-lift trucks to improve reliability. Austin Rover took up the suggestion and is already saving £30,000 each year.

QUALITY CIRCLES

The drawback of suggestion schemes is that — as presently constituted — they do not make use of the key principle of team creativity. It is an innovative system that is highly individualistic. By contrast, Quality Circles do employ team creativity. For a Quality Circle is a group of four to twelve people coming from the same work area, performing similar work, who voluntarily meet on a regular basis to identify, investigate, analyse, and solve their own work-related problems. The circle presents solutions to management and is usually involved in implementing and later monitoring them.

Each circle has a team leader. Within an organization the groups are supported and co-ordinated by a facilitator.

You can see that Quality Circles are an innovative system superimposed upon the existing structure of the organization. This has pros and cons. It could be argued that existing groups or teams, under supervisors and line managers, do not in practice engage in team creativity. Therefore it is necessary to introduce a new system designed to that end. On the other hand, adding new systems — a mini-hierarchy of Quality Circles and their leaders under facilitators who, in turn, come under co-ordinators or steering committees — offends against the principle of keeping organizations as simple as possible.

Quality Circles have flourished best in Japan. It is traditionally important in Japan to 'gather the wisdom of the people'. As we have seen the Japanese are much more creative in groups than as individuals. Some forty years ago Japanese industry was notorious for shoddy workmanship and low quality merchandise;

now Japan has one of the strongest economies in the world. There are other factors, such as a policy of long-term investment, in that success story. But the conversion of the Japanese to the gospel of quality comes high on the list. An estimated eleven million Japanese workers are organized into Quality Circles, and children are taught in school the problem-solving techniques used by Quality Circles.

SUCCESS FACTORS FOR QUALITY CIRCLES

Experience has shown that the following factors are very important for the success of Quality Circles:

● *Top leadership support.* As in the case of suggestion schemes, the most senior leader in the division, company or department has to be seen to be committed to the programme — making it clear by word and example that he or she expects all the management team to give their active support. That means committing employee time for regular circle meetings, attending circle meetings when invited and helping approved solutions to be implemented.

● *Voluntary participation.* Members and leaders are volunteers. Getting anything off the ground is much easier if people are not compelled to take part.

● *Training.* Facilitators, leaders and members are properly trained in teamwork, in problem solving and in presentation skills. At the beginning of a programme, at least the facilitator (and often the first leaders) will have been trained by a consultant or other professionally competent resource. The facilitators often subsequently train leaders and help them in turn to train their circle members.

● *Shared work background.* The first circles will have been formed by people from the same work area. This shared work knowledge helps a faster development of the essential teamwork and also helps the circle members to contain problems to those under their direct control. In manufacturing, circles are usually formed from people doing similar work but in service areas the members may be engaged in different aspects of a common process such as dealing with orders or paying invoices.

● *Solution orientated.* Circles work in a systematic way on solving problems — not just discussing them — investigating causes, looking for improvements, testing solutions and whenever possible being actively involved in implementation. The management must take care to see that suggested solutions are implemented once they have been accepted.

● *Recognition.* Circles are not paid directly for their solutions but management will arrange for proper recognition e.g. by means of visits to special events or by contributions to social functions.

The main reason why Quality Circles fail, it must be emphasized, is the lack of management support. They get off to a good start but rarely continue beyond the honeymoon period. It follows that certain criteria should be present in an organization before Quality Circles can be sucessfully introduced. The company culture should be an open one, which encourages participation. There must also be a willingness to provide the relevant facts and information to enable employees to make an informed contribution. Industrial relations must be reasonably healthy. There should be a long-term commitment on the part of management at all levels, together with a readiness to provide the necessary training resources.

TOWARDS TEAM CREATIVITY

Some companies are already developing the Quality Circles concept towards the total team creativity approach outlined above. One Scottish microelectronics firm, for example, set eighteen task teams to work on a production line problem. As a result, the line was closed for more than two weeks and a new air system was built, but the loss of time and production was minimized. 'In the old days the manager or supervisor would have wandered in and tried to do something,' said one team member. 'The whole process would have been greatly prolonged, the loss much greater.'

Suggestion Schemes and Quality Circles are really only stepping-stones leading towards the fully-fledged innovative organization. Such an organization will place a premium on creative thinking from the top downwards. It will ensure that it recruits a significant number of creative thinkers at all levels. All its organized groups — a sales team in a given region, for example — will be capable of working as a team on new ideas and innovations. The board of directors and the executive committee will in this respect lead by example, for strategic thinking calls for team creativity.

One implication will be that individuals who show promise as creative or innovative thinkers will spend some of their time outside their departments or divisions contributing as members to intellectual project groups. Set up to solve macro-problems or to explore strategic opportunities, these task teams will be interdisciplinary in nature, for diversity breeds creativity. All employees joining such an innovative organization will be fully briefed at recruitment stage as to what will be required of them in relation to innovation, including this possibility of being invited to work in project groups.

Outstandingly innovative companies, such as Digital Equipment and 3M, have led the way in this respect. Lewis Lehr emphasizes the role of teamwork in 3M in bringing a new idea to market:

> 'The whole process of commercializing a new development is *not* like a relay race — in which the scientist completes his or her lap and passes a baton to production people, who in turn run their lap and pass the baton to a sales force for the final leg of the race. Ideally there is communication and consultation among all functions at every step. They often form what we call a business development unit to exploit the new product or business ideas. Such a team may transcend the existing organization structure and be loosely formed as a matrix system.'

THE IMPORTANCE OF TRAINING AND EDUCATION

No farmer harvests from the soil unless he invests in it. To operate an innovative organization with a culture of team creativity does presuppose a trained and educated work force. Apart from technical training, everyone today needs training in the skills and techniques of effective thinking: analysing, imagining (using the brainstorming technique), valuing, and how the mind works — especially the positive part played by the unconscious mind in restructuring problems and providing solutions.

A broader education is also to be encouraged, for an innovative organization is by definition also a learning organization. Anything that stirs up, excites or trains the 10,000 million braincells of each team member is worth supporting. Visits to interesting places — not all directly work-related — can be especially rewarding. Several years ago, while viewing the King Tutankhamen exhibition in Washington's National Gallery of Art, one roving employee of Hallmark suddenly pictured the famous gold death mask as a puzzle for children. That idea paid off more than half a million dollars to the company.

The *Times* recently reported one case study in the transformation of attitudes about education and training:

A few miles south of Longbridge, at the Land Rover plant at Solihull, the assembly lines are halted for five minutes every day and for twenty minutes once a month for managers to explain to each worker what progress the company is making. Land Rover's 6,000 staff on the assembly lines operate a unique working week of four, 9¾-hour days, which allows them time to study at the company's expense everything from computer literacy to A level maths. Dozens of them have spent the extra day at the company's open learning centre, studying on the bank of video terminals. Austin Rover's similar open learning scheme also includes home study courses for subjects from healthy eating to learning to speak Japanese.

Technical improvements will mean nothing unless the product meets the customer's demands. In the past, the men on the assembly lines had no further interest in a car once it had left them. Now, Land Rover's workers are sent out in small groups to meet customers face to face. If there is a problem with the vehicle, then the production man finds out at first hand and in the most convincing fashion.

We must now visualize the innovative organization of tomorrow as *a community of creativity*. From the directors downwards every group in the organization will come to see itself as a team which is part of a yet wider team. Creative interaction will stimulate individual ideas; individual thought or reflection will in turn feed back into group meetings or into the ongoing conversation of the organization as a whole. Much more use will be made of task teams in the field of innovation. Value will be placed upon training in effective thinking skills and communication skills, upon education of the whole mind, and upon self-development within one's chosen area of work.

KEY POINTS

● Systems and structure are important, but they are only half of the matter. The other half is the people who use the systems: leadership and team membership skills, training in effective thinking and, above all, sustained commitment.

● Suggestion Schemes should have the merit of being simple. If properly managed, they are a valuable ingredient in promoting or encouraging creative thinking among the work force.

● Quality Circles do apply the principle of team creativity. As experiments, they have benefited from being voluntary. But innovative organizations should be harvesting ideas from *all* their staff. Each leader-manager should now be trained to run creative problem-solving meetings of his group, or delegate that function to a colleague with a natural aptitude for performing it.

● Training in skills and techniques is necessary, but in creative thinking a wider approach also pays off in the long-term. Education that develops the whole person, together with travel to look at other industries or to meet customers, helps to stimulate ideas and keep brains fit for innovative thinking.

● There are always reasons for not becoming an innovative organization, not least the fact that it costs money to go down that path. But can you afford the alternative?

● Innovation is more likely to come from people when their leader expects it.

> *More creativity is the only way to make tomor-*
> *row better than today.*
>
> *Anon*

10. Overcoming Resistance To Change

There is a natural opposition among men to
anything they have not thought of themselves.
                                    Sir Barnes Wallis

To innovate means to introduce or bring in something new. The word itself comes from the Latin *novus*, new, which appears in other English words such as novice, renovation and novelty. Innovation is a form of change. Change, however, is a much wider concept than innovation. For all changes are not necessarily innovations.

THE HUMAN NEED FOR CONTINUITY AND CHANGE

'The thing that has been, it is that which shall be,' said the Preacher in Ecclesiastes. 'And that which is done is that which shall be done: and there is no new thing under the sun.' The Preacher could not see anything new, whereas some of us today cannot see anything but the new. The truth lies between these extremes. Continuity and change are always present.

Our need for *both* continuity and change predisposes us to be considerably ambivalent about change. Part of our nature may see the need for it and either welcome it eagerly or accept it with resignation; the other part of our nature may deeply regret its appearance and fight against it in order to preserve the existing order. For we also have a conservative tendency. It leads us to seek to maintain existing views, conditions or institutions.

This general truth about human nature, namely that we are all attracted in varying degrees by both newness and oldness, is influenced by individual psychology. Your age, for example, is a factor. People are more inclined to change when they are younger, and they grow more conservative as they grow older. 'Young men are fitter to invent than to judge,' wrote Francis Bacon, 'fitter for execution than counsel, and fitter for new projects than settled business.'

But this generalization is riddled with exceptions. There are young men and women who have old heads on their shoulders. Equally, the fact that you have to grow older does not mean that you have to become old. When it comes to creative thinking and innovation, an old eagle is often better than a young sparrow.

How we *perceive* what is new, of course, varies from individual to individual. What is blindingly new to one person may be 'old hat' to another. But this difference may be more apparent than real. For the general concept of *newness* is like a diamond with many facets. Basically *new* describes things that have recently come into existence or use. It may be equally applied to something that is freshly made and unused (a new loaf of bread), or to something that has not been known before (a new design), or to something not experienced before (a new job.) But perhaps its most common meaning refers to being recent or original, such as something just invented, created or developed — a new book, just published, or a new tin-opener, based upon an entirely different mechanical principle.

In this latter sense the phrase 'brand new' is sometimes used for emphasis. A brand new pair of shoes, for example, is one which has just been bought. Incidentally, *new* is also used as a synonym for *fresh* in the sense of unprejudiced, such as, for example, a new (or fresh) approach to controlling pollution of the seas.

Novelty is almost the same as newness, but not quite, for it has some overtones. Novelty stresses the quality of newness. So we are inclined to call it novelty when we see or experience something that we perceive to be new, strange and unprecedented.

Bearing in mind that we like to maintain some sort of thermostatic balance between continuity and change in our lives, what appears to be novel in the sense of totally unfamiliar and totally without precedent is liable to arouse mistrust and fear. 'Man has a limited biological capacity for change,' writes Alvin Toffler. 'When this capacity is overwhelmed, the capacity is in future shock.' Again individual psychology comes into play here: what some find stimulating others will find shocking.

Cultural factors also influence our appetite for the new. Highly sophisticated, wealthy and leisured men and women may not only need new dishes to stir jaded appetites, but also large injections of novelty to stimulate their satiated minds. For many novelty is indeed like a drug, subject to the law of diminishing returns. They are also prone to the 'newer-is-truer' fallacy.

'The nature of men is greed for novelty,' wrote the Roman statesman Pliny the Elder. Larger cities and urban cultures, such as California today, breed this mental restlessness. It was evident in ancient Rome in Pliny's day, and still more so in ancient Athens. A contemporary of Pliny's, the Christian author of the Acts of the Apostles, commented: 'Now all the Athenians and the foreigners living there spent their time in nothing except telling or hearing something new.' Much later even the great Mozart fell victim to this greed for novelty. Vienna, the glittering capital of the Austrian empire in the eighteenth century was much like Rome or Athens in this respect. After *Figaro* and *Don Giovanni*, successes elsewhere, had both flopped there and after his later symphonies excited little interest a friend told Mozart: 'At first one gets acclaim and money. But after a few months the Viennese want something new.'

To summarize: both our welcoming of and our resistance to change have their roots in human nature. Broadly speaking, they stem from our partly unconscious need for a homeostatic balance between continuity and change. If we have too much change happening in our lives at any one time we tend to emphasize and preserve continuity. For too much change breeds insecurity and uncertainty: we lose our moorings in the river of time. Too much continuity, however, is equally bad. It stirs up our appetite for change. 'Such is the state of life,' wrote Samuel Johnson, 'that none are happy but by the anticipation of change. The change itself is nothing; when we have made it, the next wish is to change again.'

UNDERSTANDING THE FORCES OF RESISTANCE

It follows from the above analysis that the response to innovation is going to be very different according to the situation and the people involved. To some extent the perception by individuals of change will be governed by the social culture and corporate sub-culture in which they live and work. Western and westernized countries are generally predisposed towards change, at least since the nineteenth century. Tennyson sounded the trumpet call: 'Let the great world spin for ever down the ringing grooves of change.'

But that does not mean there is no inertia or no resistance to change. Because of our homeostatic balancing of continuity and change we may resist change that is sudden, unexpected or very great, especially if it affects us personally. As Samuel Butler wrote, 'Any very great and sudden change is death.' We may experience a kind of resurrection after it, but the actual experience of change may be perceived as painful and life-threatening.

If the change — proposed or actual — is attended with great dangers and uncertain effects, it is especially likely to arouse anxiety or fear. As Eric Hoffer writes in *The Ordeal of Change* (1964), 'We are more ready to try the untried when what we do is inconsequential. Hence the remarkable fact that many inventions had their birth as toys.'

How do you deal with the potential enemies of change? I suggest that there are five rules that need to be applied according to the needs and characteristics of the particular situation you have in mind. Let us consider each one in turn.

RULE ONE: PLOUGH UP THE GROUND

No farmer sows seeds into hard, frozen or unyielding ground. You have to prepare the way for change. Unless you can create some dissatisfaction with things as they are, you cannot induce a willingness to change. Complacency is a greater enemy to change than fear.

Go out into the highways and byways of your organization and cry out in a loud voice:

A THING IS NOT RIGHT BECAUSE WE DO IT.
A METHOD IS NOT GOOD BECAUSE WE USE IT.
EQUIPMENT IS NOT THE BEST BECAUSE WE OWN IT.

For your first target must be the assumptions and fixed ideas of the organization: the luggage it brings from its successful past. Organizations and long-established groups are like individuals in that respect. 'It is not only what we have inherited from our fathers that exists again in us,' wrote Hendrik Ibsen, 'but all sorts of old dead ideas and all kinds of old dead beliefs . . . They are not actually alive in us; but they are dormant, all the same, and we can never be rid of them.'

Therefore innovation often comes when a fresh mind, untrammelled by these dead ideas and assumptions, enters a traditional industry. Sir Henry Bessemer, the British civil engineer who invented the Bessemer Process (1856) for converting molten pig-iron into steel, once said: 'I had an immense advantage over many others dealing with the problem in as much as I had no fixed ideas derived from long-established practice to control and bias my mind, and did not suffer from the general belief that whatever is, is right.' But in his case, as with many 'outsiders', ignorance and freedom from established patterns of thought in one field were joined with knowledge and training in other fields.

Ask plenty of questions. *Why* are we doing it this way rather than any other? *What* are the criteria for success? *What* is the evidence that we are being successful? *When* did we last review these procedures? *Who* among our competitors is doing things differently and with *what* results? *Where* is the key research and development being done in this area?

These questions, repeated often, are like the points of a pneumatic drill digging up the hardened roads of organizational procedures. For you cannot sow seeds of change on tarmac roads. Organizational practices and procedures are rather like roads. 'When a road is once built,' wrote Robert Louis Stevenson, 'it is a strange thing how it collects traffic, how every year as it goes on, more and more people are found to walk thereon, and others are raised up to repair and perpetuate it, and keep it alive.'

RULE TWO: MARKET YOUR IDEAS

'In the modern world of business,' says the advertising magnate David M. Ogilvy, 'it is useless to be a creative original thinker unless you can also sell what you create. Management cannot be expected to recognize a good idea unless it is presented to them by a good salesman.'

In other words, the onus is on you to persuade others that the proposed change is a good one, bearing in mind Henry Ford's three questions: 'Is it useful? It it practicable? Is it commercial?' As money is the language of business, you have to be able to show that — at least in the middle term — the new idea or innovation will cut costs, add to profits or serve some other legitimate corporate interest. You sell ideas best by pointing out the benefits it will confer upon the 'buyer', be he an external customer or an internal member of the same organization as yourself.

In the legal sphere you are not allowed to act as judge in your own case. Your own ideas do need to be subjected to critical evaluation by others. 'New ideas can be good or bad, just the same as with old ones,' remarked Franklin D. Roosevelt. Organizations, like society at large, need to protect themselves against needless innovation, including some of your brainchildren. The 'newer-is-truer' assumption is so often found to be a false one.

In an innovative organization, with developed team creativity at work, your critics will have open minds. They will perceive the positive element in what you are proposing. They will test your ideas and, if necessary, reject them with tact. Or they may accept them and build upon them, so that the process of innovation gets underway. You can help them to see the value of a proposed change if you present it to individuals and groups with skill.

Some creative thinkers are quite adept at finding their way through the political undergrowth of the organization. Others are not so good at presenting their ideas, getting them accepted and securing the necessary resources. That is where introducing the system of *project sponsors* can be such a help. Someone high in the organization is appointed to help the innovator gain access to resources and to protect the project when it falters. It is not an easy assignment, even in such innovative organizations as 3M, as Lewis Lehr writes:

'Acting as a sponsor for an untried project is no picnic. Most sponsors, I believe, tend to bet on people rather than on products. We have a saying at 3M that, "The captains bite their tongues until they bleed." This means they have to keep their hands off the project. The first virtue of a sponsor is faith. The second is patience. And the third is understanding the differences between temporary setback and terminal problem.

'It is at this level — the level of the sponsor — that there is opportunity to plant the seeds of innovation. Make sponsoring an explicit part of the job description for every top manager. When managers come in for appraisals, they should be asked about the new projects under their wings. The economics of projects is not the first issue to raise. Stress, instead, the vision of payoff.'

In organizations which rate low in creativity and innovation, and do not appoint sponsors to act as godparents to new ideas, the process is considerably less effective and much more painful for all concerned. William James summed up one typical sequence: 'First a new theory is attacked as absurd; then it is admitted to be true but obvious and insignificant; finally it is seen to be so important that its adversaries claim that they themselves discovered it.'

RULE THREE: HAVE A PRACTICE RUN

'What is conservatism?,' asked Abraham Lincoln. 'Is it not adherence to the old and tried against the new and untried?' Men and women tend not to believe in new things until they have experience of them. Therefore why not suggest an experiment? If something is tried and tested, so that it can be matched against the present state, then it is much more likely to be accepted.

Experiment involves only limited commitment. People are usually more comfortable with that. It is only worth conducting, however, if there will be a fair and comprehensive review of the results. That does not preclude hard debate, for results are often open to several interpretations and it is important to arrive at the truth of the matter.

In the politics of innovation the proposal for a trial-run in one sector of the organization is often an acceptable compromise for the conservatives. Its drawback is the extra time it adds on to the bill. Indeed it can be used merely as a delaying tactic by those who have no intention or willingness to change. But it is always wise to assume the best motives in your adversaries. If you trust people, they may let you down; if you don't trust them, they will do you down.

'Progress is the mother of problems,' wrote G. K. Chesterton. You only have to contemplate the problems posed to us by the advance of science to see the truth of his statement. If any change is made there will be *manifest* and *latent* consequences. The manifest consequences are the ones that can be foreseen; the latent ones only emerge during or after the innovation has been made.

Sometimes hindsight shows that the innovation has not yielded the promised benefits. Perhaps the original product or service had some quality which has been lost in the improvement. In that case, if it is not too late, why not revert to the original? Hence the wisdom, if time permits, of conducting trials or experiments before adopting any innovation wholesale. Who would like to fly in a new aircraft which had not undergone rigorous test flights?

RULE FOUR: MAKE CHANGE INCREMENTAL

Inertia is not a detriment in every circumstance. It protects individuals and organizations from oversensitive response to fluctuations in conditions. Only when change — social, economic and technological — is rapid in the environment does it become a liability. For rapid change calls for rapid response.

Organizations that put their head in the sand and ignore change may find that they have to make sudden and relatively great changes in order to catch up and survive. This form of crisis management should be avoided. It arouses too much anxiety and fear about the personal consequences of change. Gradual or incremental change is much better. As we have seen, innovation should always be evolutionary rather than revolutionary. Wearing these clothes it is much less threatening.

Therefore innovation should be planned in gradual stages, as part of a continuous process of adaptation to changing circumstances. It should not be a panic response to change which is now taking an organization by the throat because yesterday that same organization failed to take it by the hand. Use the time available carefully to communicate about the need for change, experiment and review. 'Desire to have things done quickly prevents their being done thoroughly,' reflected Confucius. With innovation it is usually best to make haste slowly.

RULE FIVE: LEADERSHIP IS ESSENTIAL

'Nothing great was ever achieved without enthusiasm,' wrote Emerson. If the top leadership is not committed to and enthusiastic about change, it will not happen. Why? Because there is an element of risk in even the best prepared and planned innovation. Not all the consequences or side-effects can be foretold. There is plenty of room for uncertainty and fear. Leaders of innovation need to show moral courage, commitment and enthusiasm if they are to keep people moving on the path of progress. They should share their courage and conceal their fear.

One vital leadership skill of the chief executive is winning the commitment of others — especially the top management team — to a sustained strategy of innovation. That means first enfranchising managers to participate in strategic thinking. Then the door of decision-making must be opened at all levels so that everyone participates in *how* to implement change in so far as it affects their area of responsibility. Without implementation — making it happen — the early stages of creative thinking, research and experimental trial runs will be so much wasted effort.

*   *   *

In conclusion, change may be an untidy process, but it need not be carried out in a disorderly way. Innovation may not always turn out as planned, which may create tension. But that is not an argument against all attempts to plan and manage it. Managers who are leaders can do much to create and nurture a climate in which innovation happens. There are too many challenges and problems outside the organization awaiting attention, without leaders and managers having to expend too much time and energy overcoming negative resistance to change within it.

KEY POINTS

● People tend to be ambivalent about change. Our needs for continuity and change are homeostatically balanced. We are more likely to respond positively to change if it is gradual and not too unfamiliar or strange. Very great or sudden change tends to alarm us.

● In overcoming this natural resistance to change it is necessary first to plough up the ground. Create dissatisfaction with the way things are. Remind your organization that a person does not have to be ill in order to get better. Challenge hidden assumptions and fixed ideas. There is always a better way.

● If you cannot communicate you cannot innovate. For innovation cannot happen without a team effort, and a team or organization will not swing into action unless you and your fellow spirits persuade them to do so.

● The third rule is to offer those resisting change the possibility of an experiment. That capitalizes on our human preference for making only limited commitments before we see our way forwards clearly.

● The strength of innovation lies in its incremental nature. Innovation, in contrast to creativity, implies the accumulation of small changes across the board. Therefore, present it as a form of evolution and be content with slow but steady progress.

● Without good leadership desired change will not happen in time. Leaders need both personal qualities, notably enthusiasm, and also professional skills to involve others in decision-making and the management of change.

People support what they help to create.
Anon

CONCLUSION:
The Challenge of Innovation

*Innovation is our motto. The only trouble is
that we do not practise it.*

Anon

It is not easy to keep alive the spirit of enterprise and innovation — which implies an element of risk-taking — in business
organizations. As they get bigger and older they tend to become
more risk-averse. They cease to be enterprises, marked by bold-
ness and strenuous endeavour, and settled down into a sedentary,
comfortable middle-age of bureaucracy. This phenomenon is not
new. A worried Roman called Servaeus Africanus wrote to the
District Governor of Middle Egypt in AD288 as follows:

> 'It is apparent from the accounts alone that a number of people,
> wishing to batten on the estates of the Treasury, have invented
> titles for themselves, such as comptroller, secretary or superintend-
> ent, whereby they procure no advantage to the Treasury but swal-
> low up the profits.'

'Business is essentially about the management and marketing
of innovation and risk,' writes Professor Roland Smith, Chairman of British Aerospace. 'It is important to re-emphasize the
significance of innovation and risk to businessmen, because it
has become fashionable in Britain and Europe to talk about
rationalization and contraction.'

Rationalization, like pruning fruit trees, is relatively easy. It
usually produces short-term gains, which add to its attractions.

It consists of reducing the headcount, eliminating low margin or unprofitable product or service activities, and endeavouring to raise productivity. In other words, it focusses on loss elimination. Such benefits will be more difficult to secure in the future.

Valuable though such rationalizations are, moreover, they do not address the real agenda of the 1990s. Many technologies are now mature or declining. Therefore successful innovation is required, coupled with imaginative marketing. That in turn calls for leader-managers with a developed entrepreneurial instinct. They alone will have the will to take more calculated business risks.

The macho-management style of the 1980s is giving way to one demanding real leadership and creativity, supported by general management in depth. The successful companies of the future will be those who have developed excellence in products or services, together with the managerial leadership of sufficient quality and depth to exploit the opportunities of the world marketplace.

No innovative activity — introducing change, altering old ways of doing things, playing midwife to new ideas — can be risk-free. However carefully planned or closely calculated there is always something that has to be left to chance. You can rattle the dice for so long, but then you have to throw them.

The best chief executives and executive directors are constantly asking what is the next step. They are impatient. They love the quest for new products, new markets, new challenges and opportunities. This restless search for opportunity spurs them on.

Too many managers only reach for what is in their grasp. They do not stretch themselves or their colleagues. By hard work and by the exercise of good judgement, however, leaders demonstrate time and time again that challenging but realistic targets can be achieved. However careful or calculating in their approach to risk, they recognize when they have to commit a lot of money or resources on the basis of information which is less than complete. Seldom will it be a one-man or one-woman decision. Many meetings and consultations often take place, but at the end of the day a wise chief executive knows that all depends upon his or her ability to assess a risk in the light of the projected benefits and potential downside, and then to reach a balanced and reasonable decision. As the ancient Greek proverb says, 'Chance fights ever on the side of the prudent.'

It is essential for business leaders, then, to accept the risk-element in decision-making, especially when it comes to innovation. Risk means the possibility of loss or injury. But if you never go out on a limb you will not pluck the best fruit.

In a world where there is an irreducible element of chance or luck it is inevitable that some projects or enterprises will not succeed. It is no use worrying about possible failure. The leader-manager is not paid to worry: his or her job is to resolve and decide. Worry prevents you from doing that. As one chief executive said to me, 'Worry is nothing more than a substitute for action or a failure to recognize that there is no course of action open. It may be a result of failure to think things through, or fear of finding out. If unchecked it would consume a chief executive's energy, confuse his thinking or force him into something he shouldn't do at all.'

But an element of worry is unavoidable in life: at least it keeps you awake. The fact that you have learnt to handle worry does not remove it. There are two important principles. First, let the worry precede the decision rather than follow it. As an Arab proverb says, 'Men sleep well in the Inn of Decision.' Secondly, no leader is privileged to worry aloud or in public. People are always watching. Undue concern, uneasiness or panic can spread like wildfire. School yourself to act as if nothing is happening. Calm, confident and collected leadership creates a climate which is conducive to success.

If failure occurs, how does the organization respond? Organizations which fear failure so much that they establish all sorts of controls to ensure that it does not happen do not have that problem. Unfortunately they do not have many successes either. They have condemned themselves to mediocrity.

A chief executive of a company was recently summoned to the corporate headquarters of the international group for whom he worked. He had just made a substantial loss on a major project and therefore he was expecting to be dismissed. At the end of his meeting with the President, however, neither the loss nor his imminent departure had been mentioned. As he stood up to leave he said, 'It's good to know I have still got a job. I must confess I thought you would fire me today as a result of that substantial loss.'

'Fire you?' replied the President. 'Hell, no, your education has just cost me one million dollars!'

Provided that failure is not the consequence of recklessness or incompetence, innovative organizations will not exact revenge or make scapegoats. It is usually easy to be wise after the event. Although you should endeavour to be wise before the decision, it is no good belabouring yourself for not knowing then what you know now. Put it down to experience in your ledger of successes and failures. As they say, you can't win them all. Oscar Wilde once defined experience as the name we give to our mistakes.

It all comes back to the real commitment and leadership of the chief executive and the top management team. If they are firmly resolved upon profitable growth through team creativity, then the challenge of innovation will be met. Even with a good track record, do not leave anything to chance. Certainly, the best way to lose an innovative edge is to spend too much time admiring a successful past. A good reputation is history, nothing more. Good companies must always search for excellence.

KEY POINTS

● To innovate is not to reform: it is introducing useful change. Because innovations are new and untried (or only partially tried) they carry risks of various kinds. For humans, as Benjamin Franklin said, 'the way to be safe is never to be secure.'

● The essence of business is trading for profit. Profits are really the wages you are paid for innovating and taking risk within a social capitalist economy.

● An innovative organization has to learn to live with risk. Risk cannot be justified, however, if no one bothered to weigh or calculate it. To underestimate risk sometimes signals lack of experience or judgement, but to ignore risk altogether is plain foolhardiness.

● Entrepreneurial business leaders have to be able to assess risk and make decisions in conditions where all the information is not available. That is why they make good innovators. 'Few moments are more pleasing,' wrote Samuel Johnson, 'than those when the mind is concerting measures for a new under-taking.'

He who dares nothing, need hope for nothing.

English Proverb

Index